To Vanessa

my new love

Bobmi B

2021.

NEARLY 79
LAUGHTER AND LOSS

First Edition published 2019 by 2QT Limited (Publishing)
Settle, North Yorkshire BD24 9RH United Kingdom

Book Design by Charlotte Mouncey

Photographs, watercolour paintings and drawings by Robert McBurney

Publisher Disclaimer: The events in this memoir are described according to
the Author's recollection; recognition and understanding of the events and
individuals mentioned are in no way intended to mislead or offend.
As such the Publisher does not hold any responsibility for any inaccuracies
or opinions expressed by the author. Every effort has been made to
acknowledge and gain any permission from organisations and persons
mentioned in this book. Any enquiries should be directed to the author.

Printed in Great Britain by TJ International Ltd.

A CIP catalogue record for this book is available from the British Library

ISBN - 978-1-912014-36-1

NEARLY 79
LAUGHTER AND LOSS

Robert McBurney

2QT
PUBLISHING

In gratitude to family and friends

WINSOR ORANGE   ALIZARIN

AVIGNON ORANGE   PERYLENE MAROON

INTRODUCTION

This book began as a diary, which I started at Christmas 2017 when I was ill. Writing about day-to-day events stirred memories of my childhood and, as a result, alongside the diary I began to write memoir pieces.

I continued with the diary, not with any real discipline but in a rather haphazard way, writing when I had something to say. I decided to give myself a deadline of July 13, which was my seventy-ninth birthday. This led to my title.

Finally I arrived at the point where I had seven months of diary entries and about fifty 'discrete' chapters of memoir. I suppose that I could have kept the two elements separate but I decided, as a way of changing pace, to alternate monthly groups of diary entries with small sections of memoir. I've described the memoir chapters as being 'discrete' because each of them is complete, rather as a poem or a short story might be.

Though the memoir chapters are in historical order and the diary entries are chronological, no effort has been made to link the pieces into a coherent narrative.

In essence, this book is a collection of writings. In culinary terms one might liken it to a box of chocolates rather than a sherry trifle – though one or two of the chocolates have a hard centre. I like to think that it can be read conventionally or, just as easily, 'dipped' into and read in any order.

Following this page is a preface, which I wrote to introduce myself. On re-reading it I am embarrassed by the degree of 'me' 'me' 'me' which it contains. In Yorkshire we'd say, 'He's a bit up himself.'

I hope not.

PREFACE

Accidentally me. I was born in July 1939. Not a moment too soon it seems, because shortly afterwards the house in which I was born disappeared under an ICI chemical works.

My mother used to tell me that my birth was traumatic for us both. She may have been exaggerating but she did say that I was popping in and out over a period of three or four days. Sometimes I think that I might have had a premonition of what was to come.

So eventually I was launched into this world in which a series of chance happenings, good and bad, have determined the course of my life. As I look back, I realise how little I have had to do with the pivotal events that have affected me. I've been carried along, sometimes willingly, occasionally not. Chance events have shaped me, as they shape us all.

My childhood was often unhappy. On reflection I can see how dysfunctional our family was. We moved from village to village. We were poor but affected superiority. Alcohol and gambling cast a dark shadow over our lives.

I went to Ripon Grammar School as a day boy. I was bright. Despite missing several weeks through illness, I came second in the intake at the end of the first year. I was given a scholarship to the boarding school. I was a complex, screwed-up child and I was badly bullied. I was covered in bruises for a couple of years. I lived in despair. From then on, my academic achievements took a steady nose dive and I left school at sixteen.

I had several clerical jobs, some of which I've written about. National Service was coming to its end and, as most boys were called up in their late teens, I thought that I had missed it. I was amazed when I was conscripted, despite being nearly twenty-one years old.

Half-hoping to be rejected, I remember standing stripped to my underwear in a lofty room somewhere in Bradford. I stood in a queue behind a boy who was sweetly ripe with body odour and mastoids. He was applying for the third time. I don't know what happened to him but, needless to say, they took me. I became an officer cadet.

They said that I commanded men with a pleasant authority. I am less sure about that. Admittedly, when it came to solving military challenges such as getting six men across a deep ditch with nothing more than a length of string, a plank, a barrel and a bowler hat, I displayed ingenuity. Apart from that, I think they were being kind. I was commissioned as best cadet and posted to the headquarters of the Royal Army Service Corps in Aldershot. Suddenly I was exposed to a life of privilege and ceremony.

Although I did everything that I could to make a success of my National Service, the very accident of being called up proved to be a significant event in my life.

Years later, having left the army, when I was struggling with a hand-to-mouth existence as a commercial photographer, I was invited to join a photographic advertising studio. Almost entirely because of that fortuitous and unexpected event I was able to move on eventually and create my own group of companies involved in advertising photography, design and stock pictures.

From a personal point of view, I'm the eldest of five. I have been married three times and I'm happy to say that I still love and like my two ex-wives. I am very happily married now, but so much of this book concerns my younger life that I don't talk much about my wife Sue, my children, her children and our grandchildren. However, without them I would probably be a grumpy old man and quite unable to write.

I have had a wonderful life, full of humour and occasional sorrow.

I'm quite obsessive and there is no doubt that I'm a bit geeky. Who knows – it's probably something to do with those first four days of 'popping in and out'.

I paint, I draw, I photograph, I design, I build boats and furniture. I cook, I read, I'm pretty 'close' with Bach, I laugh at my own jokes. In company I get excited and I talk too much. I love Ruby, my Border Terrier.

Life is just full of things to do! Now it seems that, almost by chance, I have become a writer. Also completely by chance I live in Leeds, another accident but one that has lasted for forty years.

Contents

INTRODUCTION 7

PREFACE 9

Tyers Hall 18
Kiln Hill 20
Lady Cecilia 25
Bows and Arrows 30
Dad 31
Aglionby Street 38

Diary - December 2017 44

The Wooden Chest 54
Silver Glider 56
Joe and Me 58
Sunny Bank Hall 63
The Duck 67
Eleven Plus 69

Diary - January 2018 72

Ripon Grammar School 100

Cadet Camp 103
Waiting for Benskin 109
The Company Medical 112
General Accident Fire and Life Assurance Corporation -
The Office 115
Pipe Smoking 118

Diary - February 2018 122

National Service Commission 128
Headquarters Subaltern 131
The Wedding Invitation 134
Mons Officer Cadet School 137
Mark 1 Land Rover 139
The Alvis 143

Diary - March 2018 150

Oliver's Zip 170
Resignation 172
Rude Awakenings, Civilian Life 175
Taxi Driving 178
Phobia 183
Kenneth Michael 188

Diary - April 2018 200

Kenneth's Ashes 216
Walking in County Cork 218

Northern Rock..224
The Gaiety...225
Voyage to Whitby...228
Flash Powder..234

Diary - May 2018...240

Dad's Final Illness..254
Learning to Ride a Bike..257
North Sea Crossing...260
Limericks..265
Peter Peter..267
Fishing with John...270
Selling the Saab..273

Diary - June 2018...278

The Birthday Party..288
Exhibition...290
Turkey Soup..293
Maisie...297
Diamond and Maya..301
Bach..302
The Wart...303

Diary - July 2018..308

Thanks..319

Memories
Early Childhood

Tyers Hall

I think it must have been near the end of the Second World War that we lived at Tyers Hall near Barnsley. I remember it as a big stone house divided into three homes. We rented the middle one. The central front door was approached by a substantial flight of stone steps.

In those days, there were no toys to buy. Everything had to be cobbled together out of whatever was to hand. I had a bright-red wooden car on a pram chassis, which I imagine had been made by a friend of my father.

One summer evening my sister Mary, who was two years younger than me, helped to push me and my car down the front steps. I remember that it wasn't a comfortable ride as the car grounded on each step. Mary was only a toddler and not very effective at pushing. Even so, we got to the bottom of the steps, at which point I slipped forward and my knees jammed under the wooden bonnet. My mother tried to free me but I was stuck.

'Daddy will be home soon,' said Mummy. True enough, shortly afterwards, holding an axe in one hand and a saw in the other, my father came round the corner of the building. Despite being only four or five years old, I knew that my father, wearing his business suit, was not a practical man. I also knew that I was in a serious situation and that, in order to release me from my car, my father would have to cut off my legs. Because it was him, I knew that it wouldn't hurt.

Never for a second did I think that he would hit my car, which I loved beyond measure. When he hit it with the axe, it took me a moment or two to understand what was happening. I cannot remember any more of this story, nor can I pretend it was the death of innocence. But it must have been a beginning.

Kiln Hill

I am the eldest of five children. My sister Mary is two
years younger than me, followed by Kenneth Michael,
who died eleven years ago. Fourth is Margaret, whom
I scarcely know as she went to Australia on one of the
£10 assisted passages with her husband, Ron, when she
was a teenager. Finally there is Louise, who is seventeen
years younger than me and the baby of the family, though
she is also the keeper of the family's history and possibly
its most energetic member. Writer, poet, artist, printer,

wonderful cook and, if I remember correctly (though she might wish me to forget), a one-time Egyptian belly-dancing enthusiast.

Mary and I played together as a team when we were little and when Ken came along a couple of years later we did boss him around quite a lot. He was always small and slightly built; if Mary and I were 'cowboys', Ken was always the 'Indian'.

At this time, we lived at Kiln Hill near Pateley Bridge. It was an old farmhouse without gas or electricity, which we rented. My mother, Maisie, cooked on primus stoves and we had open fires and oil lamps. Bedtime was by torchlight with stone hot-water bottles, which were responsible for vicious blisters. We would wrap the water bottles in shawls or towels, but somehow we still managed to get burned. We would frighten ourselves by shining the torches through our fingers and imagining ever more fearsome dragons on the bedroom walls. I remember that the beds were so cold that they felt wet.

The house adjoined a paddock with stabling and a barn and we rented the nearest stable, in which we kept Percy the pig. The stable door was in two parts so that the top part could be opened without Percy being able to escape. At feeding time we would peer into the stall. Percy was invariably in the very far corner with his back to us; he would give the impression of being deeply involved in some piggy thing and quite unaware of us. We would pick up the pail, open the bottom door quietly and go in. As we entered, Percy would spin round and burst past us before we could close the door. He would then do several laps of the paddock, running hard and leaning into the bends. Finally he would head for the horse trough and sink his snout deeply into the water like a thoroughbred. He would take deep draughts of water. This happened almost every day – particularly when we children were on duty. The thinking of the day was that pigs shouldn't drink water but it should be part of their food. Consequently, Percy grew leaner and fitter. I don't think he ever put on much weight; his food was probably of poor quality as things were in short supply for us all. Mary may remember what happened to him. Fortunately I cannot.

In the far corner of the paddock in the last stall lived the bull. He belonged to the farmer. He escaped surprisingly often. I don't know if he was dangerous but he was big, and his presence was a constant menace to us. The cry would go up 'The bull's out!' He would trot across the paddock and, with his head down and his horns underneath it, he would lift the very substantial five-barred field gate off its hinges so that it dropped onto his back. Then he would trot out from underneath it and head off down the road. Farmhands from nearby farms would appear and eventually the bull would be returned to his stall. He had a ring through his nose; once they got a hook through that, he was easy to handle. When I think about it now it seems so sad. Had he been with cows, no doubt he would have been happy and docile. I do remember that it took several men to lift the gate back onto its hinges.

The next time I got close to such a big beast was in Aldershot, when we were taken to the military slaughterhouse and I saw a steer being killed. A captive bolt pistol was put against its forehead and fired. The steer's legs folded violently against its belly with a loud 'thwack', and for a moment it hung in mid-air before it crashed to the ground. The shock of instant death was huge. I never saw a movement quite like that again until, on a TV programme, I saw Joe Frazier being hit by Mohammed Ali in one of their fights. Joe's legs kicked up behind him and he seemed to jump in the air. It was the same involuntary reaction to the effect on his central nervous system.

He fought on. Astonishing bravery. (Or, Sue says 'foolhardiness'!)

Despite my own tall and gangling figure, I once had to fight three three-minute rounds during military training. I was fitter than I've ever been and I was matched against a much shorter, slightly plump man of the same weight. We must have looked very odd. The result is not important but, at the end of three rounds, I could not hold my hands above my waist. My exhaustion was complete. How fighters go for so long at such pace, throwing and receiving punches whilst remaining on their feet, is amazing. It's easy for those of us who always had other career options to criticise boxing. Accepting the dangers, nothing detracts from the bravery of those who step into the ring and, often after months of training and social privation, put their bodies and reputations on the line in the most public way.

Lady Cecilia

When Maisie, my mother, was a young girl of six or seven years of age, she and her mother went to live in the house of Wilfred Roberts, the son of Lady Cecilia Roberts.

Wilfred Roberts' wife had died shortly after childbirth in 1924. He was now living at his house in Easby, Cumberland, with his new baby daughter and he needed someone to look after her.

Maisie's mother, my Nana, was a qualified nurse. She accepted the role on condition that her own daughter could accompany her. From all that I could learn from Maisie, what followed was undoubtedly one of the happiest periods of her life.

Shortly after arrival at Easby, Maisie was sent to a school at Lanercost, close to the family's estate. However, she was taken out from the school quite hurriedly when Nana learned that the children were lined up routinely and smacked. After this, Lady Cecilia took over Maisie's education.

Every working day Lady Cecilia's old chauffeur-driven car collected Maisie from Wilfred Roberts' house and took her a short distance to Lady Cecilia's house in the nearby village of Boothby. There, in Lady Cecilia's study, Maisie learned French and reading, and they painted watercolours together.

From Maisie's account, and from what I have read, Lady Cecilia seems to have been an extraordinarily vibrant personality. Her husband had been Under-Secretary of State for India and, having lived there for some years, she favoured Indian clothing. Most of her clothes had been handmade for her in India and she wore these on a daily basis. Maisie has told me that Lady Cecilia had an elaborate, tall headdress that she wore with her colourful costumes at dinner parties. Her long clothing nearly (but not quite) disguised the fact that she wore her gardening shoes underneath. The shoes could be seen when she walked but, this aside, the total effect was very striking.

Lady Cecilia was passionately temperate regarding alcohol. Tea was served on all occasions. Lady Cecilia poured the tea herself. I don't know whether or not she included lemon or milk or sugar, but I do know that her guests were not invited to make requests. She knew how tea should be drunk and, as Maisie said to me, 'You drank what you were given.'

Wilfred's wife had kept two lovebirds in the house at Easby. Knowing nothing of caged birds, Maisie thought that this was very cruel. Shortly after her arrival at the house, she opened the cage door and allowed the birds to fly away. She remembers how kind Wilfred was in not saying anything, though one can easily imagine that the loss of his wife's birds, so soon after the loss of his wife, must have added to his pain.

Of Wilfred, Maisie says that he was sweet, nice and kind. He would take her for walks accompanied by a 'gingery' sheepdog. She said, 'He had an office in the house and therefore he must have done some work for the estate,' though mostly she remembers him walking around aimlessly smoking his pipe.

On occasion, Lady Cecilia would take Maisie out in the car. They would visit exhibitions and friends and the estate farms and cottages. It seems that Lady Cecilia became very fond of Maisie; in turn, Maisie loved her like a grandma.

Lady Cecilia's eldest daughter Winifred (the artist) was married to Ben Nicholson (the artist), and they lived in a farmhouse called Bankside, which was only a short distance away from the family home in Boothby. Maisie described Winifred as tall, slim and very pretty with dark hair. 'She would sit on a chair and paint whilst I sat on the stool next to her.'

Winifred would say of her mother that she couldn't give enough time to painting because she was so busy organising events such as carol singing and plays and parties. Indeed, amongst other diversions, Maisie remembers taking part in an Indian Nativity play.

I think that Maisie spent quite a lot of time with Winifred and Ben Nicholson. She always said that she learned to paint at Ben's knee. She described him as 'a very ordinary man', though she told me that he insisted on large windows being fitted in the farmhouse to flood his studio with light, so it does sound as if he had a clear idea of his artistic worth early in his career.

Maisie remembers him painting bunches of grapes and the garden at Easby. She also remembers him painting the red train that ran in the valley near the farmhouse. She said that you could see the railway from the top of the house. She remembers the picture hanging 'behind the fireplace in the morning room at Boothby'.

It seems that when Ben was asked what he was painting he invariably replied, 'Ginger biscuits.'

At one point, Ben gave Maisie a pile of drawings with instructions to draw on the back of them as he no longer needed them.

I think that Maisie and Nana lived with the family for three or four years. Whilst she had an extraordinary recall of detail of people and places, Maisie was less sure of dates during our conversations. She talked about Wilfred's daughter, 'A beautiful little girl with curly blonde hair,' whom she felt was almost her baby sister.

Suddenly, with no warning, no explanation and no chance even to say goodbye, Maisie was taken away from Easby by Nana.

Maisie described Nana as a selfish mother intent on her own career and with little care for her daughter. She also thought that Nana was jealous of the bond that existed between Lady Cecilia and herself. It seems that the rest of the staff actively disliked Nana as she thought that she was superior to them. Also, by this time Wilfred Roberts intended to remarry, so there could have been any number of reasons for her hasty departure. Whatever those reasons, Maisie was heartbroken. Even in her nineties, she was visibly upset.

She said to me, 'I can see it all in my head. I can see the way the twigs grew on the trees and the blossoms. I can see it all. They belonged to me. That little girl, I loved her, I thought she was mine. I loved Lady Cecilia, I thought she was mine. How could they take me away like that?'

From that time on, Maisie lived with relations and eventually with her Granny Whittaker in a cottage in Wetheral beside the River Eden. It was a beautiful place that Maisie grew to love and where, a few years ago, Louise and I scattered her ashes.

Bows and Arrows

I think that the large white sow with a litter of piglets must have been in a pen at the back of the paddock. Almost certainly she belonged to the farmer Fred Hawley, who I think was our landlord.

I was in hunting mode. Admittedly it was me who held the bow and I'm sure that there was a degree of wishful thinking as I imagined myself in the wilds of America, hunting to survive; but I was not at the time, nor am I now, aware of loosing the arrow. I think that the arrow was tipped with a needle tied on with thread because it stuck in the top of the sow's flank and waved about. She squealed at the top of her voice and raced around her pen, followed by a large number of anxious piglets.

I remember how desperate I felt. I had to get the arrow back. With Mary's help, I decided that if we held Kenneth upside down by his feet over the pen he should be able to snatch the arrow as the sow ran past. Understandably Kenneth didn't like this idea, but his protests were ignored and we held him there for several laps until the arrow was retrieved. I remember that he made almost as much noise as all the pigs combined. Poor little man.

Dad

Some of my earliest memories are of my mother Maisie pleading with my sister Mary and me to 'be good' because daddy was coming home soon and 'I don't want him to be cross with us'.

This was often said and, whatever the rights or wrongs of Maisie's parenting, we felt very protective of her and responsible for her safety. We really felt that it was us versus him.

I think that the problems between my father Kenneth and me began when I, as a young child, stood up to him in defence of my mother. I remember an incident where my mother was crying helplessly and I was hot and flushed with tears after trying to stop my father bullying her.

It is probable that my father was jealous of my mother's relationship with me, but equally I think he found it difficult to forgive any challenge to his authority. I believe it was from then on that my father began to find reasons for disliking me.

My father was tall, well-set and good-looking and also a very complex man. His mother, Gwendolyn, was the eldest daughter of a middle-class family. When her mother died young, Gwendolyn was obliged to take over the running of the household. Her younger siblings all went to university and later to professional careers, which she was denied.

When she had her own two boys, Kenneth and Reginald, she was determined that they would go to university. Her husband, my grandad, was relatively uneducated and I think that she was the driving force behind her boys' education. I do not know about Reggie as a young man, but in adulthood he had a successful career in educational publishing in Canada. I know that my father said (of himself) that he resented going to university, where he read physics, and that he would have liked to be a mechanic. From all that I knew of him, he had no practical aptitudes whatsoever and this ambition always surprised me. My sister Mary says that he told her that he would have liked to be an actor. I have some pictures of him at university as the 'lead' in Gilbert and Sullivan costume, and he certainly looks very handsome and happy.

After my father's death, I was shocked to learn that he had been married previously to the daughter of an eminent Halifax family. She divorced him for infidelity. In the early 1930s this must have sent shockwaves through everyone who knew about it, particularly my father's parents.

I already knew that, at some time before meeting my mother, my father had driven his car off a precipitous bank near Halifax. It has been said, and never denied, that he did this deliberately. His injuries were so severe that he spent many months in hospital before being discharged with one shoulder two inches lower than the other. My mother told me that a 'bar girl' was involved, and I think she mentioned a pregnancy.

There can be no doubt that, prior to meeting Maisie, my father suffered several shattering upheavals in his life. It was only after his death, and knowing of his previous marriage, that I could begin to try and understand his complex character and how these early experiences must have affected him.

Putting it bluntly, the father that I knew was often emotionally cruel. His life, (and therefore our lives), was marred by drunkenness, gambling and his frequent infidelity.

We moved from village to village because of his behaviour. Our lives were ones of constant upheaval. He gambled compulsively and it seemed that we never had any money. He often sold the furniture; sometimes he sold the house.

He would never accept gifts. We were not allowed to celebrate his birthday or give him Christmas presents. Once, when we were little, he came home late on Christmas

Eve and unwrapped all the Christmas presents before re-wrapping them in newspaper. Drink played a large part in his life and there were many painfully embarrassing moments, particularly when we were teenagers.

Once, when I was eleven, five years after the end of the Second World War when anti-German feeling was still running high, he said to me in anger that I was no better than a 'German Hun Dog'. I don't remember the circumstances but I remember the bitterness with which he spoke.

As teenagers, we begged Maisie to leave him.

When apart from his family, he could be charming. Strangers who met him would think so.

During the war he was a civil servant with an influential position. I have a letter of thanks addressed to him, which indicates that he had a pivotal position in organising and arranging accommodation for some of the 17,500 RAF civilian workers who were involved in the construction of Lancaster bombers at the Avro works in Yeadon, Yorkshire. He told me that after the war he was invited to stay on with the Ministry, but the lure of being his own boss with the freedom that might offer was too tempting.

Most of his working life was spent as a manufacturer's agent. This meant that he spent long periods away from home, which was probably a relief for Maisie though in truth I think she always loved him and she must have wondered what he was doing.

In his later working years, he taught Mathematics and English as a Second Language to students in Bradford. His students liked him and, in that role, he found some purpose and reward.

In his retirement he seemed diminished. He walked to the local pub every evening and drank three pints of bitter. If for some reason he only had two pints, he told me quite seriously that he would have an extra one the following evening.

He kept accurate records of his petrol consumption and, with a view to its part-exchange value, he would stop using his car altogether if he reached the average mileage for the year (as stated in *Glass's Guide*) before the anniversary date.

I think he dreamed of escape. Though he had no intention of buying anything, he would often walk to a local garage and gaze at camper vans and caravans.

Throughout my adult life I was aware that he was uncomfortable in my presence and in later years he would try to avoid me.

As a child, you don't recognise dysfunction in your own family. Dysfunction is the norm. When finally you are able to recognise it, certainly in my case, the sense of betrayal makes you very angry. There can be little doubt that in my teenage and early adult years I was outspoken in my criticism of my father. In later years I tried to hold him closer, but without success. Even physically, he would shudder if I attempted to hug him.

Quite late in his life, he wrote two incredibly bitter letters to me. He was obsessed with money and one of these letters concerned £5, which he said that I had owed to him for nearly twenty-five years.

By this time I was relatively well off. I knew nothing of this debt. I couldn't bear to think that my father had been dwelling on it for so long; that something which was so inconsequential to me had become all-consuming to him. It was easy to give him the money but I was deeply upset. I asked my mother if she knew about the letter. She was saddened, but said that my father couldn't help himself. I suspect that his bitterness was not only about the money.

Even at the end of his life, we couldn't really make contact. When he was ill and in bed, I tried to hold his hand but he pulled it away. Later, in defence of us both, Louise said that his skin was probably tender.

Often children blame themselves for their parent's failings and, in my own case, I know that I was arrogant and hurtful. Even at the age of seventy-eight years, I wish that I could go back and change things. I desperately wish that things had been different.

My father died in 1990. I am writing this in 2018 and I've been trying to take a longer and hopefully more thoughtful view of his life as I knew it. In the hope of understanding him better, I've given weight to the reality of the toxic combination of nature and nurture that he experienced, and which undoubtedly shaped his personality and behaviour. As I write these words 'nature' and 'nurture', I laugh ruefully.

What, I think, do they say about me?

After fifty years of heavy wine drinking and impulsive behaviour how fit am I to sit in judgement?

What will my children write about me?

Aglionby Street

My first memory of Nana is when she lived at 29 Aglionby Street, Carlisle, where she ran a boarding house. She had two permanent lodgers, Mr Hickson, a bank manager, and Auntie Marjorie, who was a primary-school teacher. They were both single and, to the best of my recollection, they came home for lunch every day. Mr Hickson was a gruff man who rarely spoke. His face was heavily carbuncled. It seems that once, when I was a little boy, I kissed him on the cheek. This startled him considerably. Maisie, who never forgot this, said, 'I don't think he had ever been kissed before.'

Nana kept a knitting needle on the table with which to rap small hands that might reach out without asking first. Meals were taken in the semi-basement which was divided into two rooms, the front room with a long dining table and a back room which was a kitchen. A serving hatch connected the two.

One day I was in the kitchen alone just before lunch was served. I saw Nana's cat eating custard by dipping its foot into the jug and then licking it.

I went into the dining room and rather primly (and certainly unwisely) told everyone what I had seen. Faced with the possibility of having to make more custard, maybe even having to 'do without' because of a shortage of ingredients, Nana made the unforgivable choice of calling me a liar. I protested; she insisted. Despite any discomfort that they might have felt, Mr Hickson and Auntie Marjorie both knew where the power lay and they ate the custard.

A small event for adults, but a lifetime memory for a child.

Nana, despite her firmness, was kind to many people. She would 'take in' old people who were dying, also pregnant girls who in those days might have nowhere else to go. I remember us going into a bedroom to see an old man who had died in the night. Nana closed his eyes and put pennies on them. His face was thin and his skin was waxen. It was the first time I'd seen a body and, as Nana said, there was nothing to be frightened of.

In the evenings Marjorie, Nana and a woman friend who also lived in Aglionby Street would play Solo. I played with them and I remember their laughing concern when once I declared a 'Misère Ouverte' which, true to my form at the time, I didn't 'make'.

We children spent most of our summer holidays at Nana's. She would usually buy a new outfit of clothes for me, which must have been an enormous help to my parents who were invariably short of money.

I used to go fishing in the local River Eden. One evening when I walked down to the river, I met two men who were 'bobbing' for eels. Even so long ago, I think they were men of a dying breed. They had a long pole with a short length of rope on the end that led to a mop head of worms. The worms were threaded lengthways onto lengths of knitting wool, several to a strand, each strand about a foot long. The strands were gathered at one end and tied onto the rope. The mop was used at night; it was lowered into dark corners of the water, behind rocks and under the bridge.

Eels have backward-facing teeth; once they have taken hold of a worm, their teeth tangle with the wool and they can be lifted out.

I didn't stay with the men to witness the fishing because, though they were friendly enough, they were very rough in appearance and certainly Nana would have expected me home before dark.

Eels are fascinating creatures. I have caught several, mostly whilst fishing for other species. They can grow to a considerable size. Years ago, I read about a huge specimen caught in Victorian times, trapped by its girth in a drain off the Thames. It was put on display in an aquarium and lived for several years.

Eels can swim as powerfully backwards as forwards. When you catch them they twist about your line covering everything in slime, though as they grow bigger the slime disappears. To a small boy they seemed very sinister, lurking in the deep dark water. Indeed, they are mysterious creatures, travelling across land and oceans during their lifetime. When put down on grass, they twist and writhe dramatically; put them on newspaper and they lie quite still. If you pick one up between three fingers, so that the central finger presses down slightly between the other two and causes a kink in the eel's body, it will become rigid like a poker. I have read this though I've never tried it.

The slime and the sharp teeth have rather put me off.

Diary

23rd December 2017–
1st January 2018

December 2017

Saturday 23rd

Pneumonia and fever prevent me from sleeping.

I've been looking at some of Stewart Lowdon's watercolour paintings online. They are small, 8x5 inches, and loosely impressionistic. They glow like jewels. Stewart Lowdon travelled and painted in Greece, and one can see that the paintings were made on the spot: simple scenes of archways, cottages and harbours with very little evidence of preparatory drawing. Mostly drawing with the brush, though the sheer line of the boats is sharp enough to suggest a quick pencil. Solid geometry underlining all, which in turn makes everything else, however loose, credible. I've begun to realise that paintings like these give us access to dreams. Certainly, they are representative but had the representation been more literal we would always be dragged back to the subject and to the detail.

In the early hours I telephone 111. Despite long lists of questions, the service is very good, and eventually I see a doctor at 8am. I'm prescribed antibiotics and directed to an all-night chemist in Bradford quite close to the surgery.

Sue is driving and she goes into the chemist's shop. On her return she tells me that the shop is small and overcrowded, all the signs and notices are in Urdu, the man behind the counter is really lovely and the shop is open twenty-four hours a day seven days a week. Despite her enthusiasm and my interest, I am glad to get home to bed.

Sunday 24th – Thursday 28th

Christmas passes in a daze. Sue becomes ill and at lunchtime on Thursday has a home visit from Dr Hickman from our local surgery. He confirms that Sue has pneumonia. Dr Hickman must be one of everybody's favourite doctors but, as he leaves, I thank him using the name 'Shipman'. As I return to the house, I'm aware of the enormity of my mistake, though it takes me a moment or two to convince myself that I actually said it. When I realise what I've done, I try to draw comfort from the fact that I was speaking to his departing back. He didn't flinch and it's just possible that he didn't hear me.

I go into the bedroom and tell Sue and my daughter Stevie. At first, they don't believe me, and then they laugh. What is almost worse is that they don't seem surprised. I hope that Dr Hickman, if he heard me, is equally charitable and will, like my family, excuse me on the grounds of age and excitement at his visit.

Friday 29th

Snow.

A page on the BBC website says, 'Turkey crackdown pushes intellectuals out.' So soon after Christmas, I struggle with this concept for a moment or two.

Saturday 30th

At about 1am, Sue wakes me to tell me that she cannot swallow. In a futile effort, I encourage her to swallow liquid and to try and swallow her antibiotics. She is coughing horribly and eventually an ambulance takes us to A&E in St James's Hospital in Leeds. We arrive at about 6am and spend the rest of the day there. As one would expect of the heroic NHS staff, despite the pressure they are caring and thoughtful. Eventually Sue is seen by a doctor who is concerned by the swelling in her throat and prescribes antibiotics, fluids and steroids intravenously, plus oxygen. We are told that she will be transferred to the ENT ward in Leeds General Infirmary and so begins a long wait.

There is so much of interest in an A&E department. Some of the ambulance women were particularly striking. Tall and athletic, looking purposeful in their tight cargoes and boots, they might have been extras in *A Space Odyssey*. They moved through the room with perfect balance, despite turning and talking as they went. As a boxer would say, the power comes from the legs. The men, on the other hand, were less graceful. Possibly the upper body strength of men affects their centre of gravity.

Trolleys were side by side. Suddenly Sue alerted me to the patient on the trolley behind me. I turned and saw a man lying on his side in the foetal position, balanced precariously on the nearside handrail of his trolley. A man I assumed to be his partner was reaching across and trying to hold him. The patient was sliding towards me; he was quite inert and, had I not taken his weight, he would have fallen to the floor. His partner came around to my side and took over. I felt very sorry for him and, patting him on the shoulder, I asked him if he was okay. Strangely, he seemed slightly irritated.

Later I saw him pushing the trolley on the far side of the department. The patient was still in the same foetal position; he seemed young and possibly handsome, though he looked as if he needed a shave. I thought that his clothing was dishevelled. Sue's memory of him is different. She says that he was well dressed in a coat of many colours, and that he was slightly built. My impression was that he was powerfully built. How interesting that we should see things so differently. We both remember that his eyes were wide open but he gave no evidence of any awareness of his surroundings. On reflection, I think his partner was probably his carer.

Eventually hospital transport transferred Sue to an assessment ward in Leeds General Infirmary, where she was to wait for a bed in ENT. I came home to get some of her clothes and then sat with her whilst she was examined by doctors and a consultant. The steroids were doing their job and the swelling in her throat had reduced. She could now talk in a hoarse whisper. The swelling was close to her airways and was a cause for concern. Surprisingly, given the number of people in A&E, Sue was the only person in the assessment ward. Eventually I left and came home. Later she phoned me to say that a bed had been found; she was in the ENT ward and expected to stay there for forty-eight hours.

Sitting with Sue brought back memories of my own time in a busy, mixed, assessment ward some years previously. An older Irishwoman, Mrs Doherty, statuesque even whilst lying down, was brought into the ward on a trolley from which porters tried to move her onto a bed. She was very unhappy and very vocal. At the top of her voice she accused the porters of lusting after her and of inappropriate touching. There were two of them and they took it in turns to approach her before being beaten off. Despite her distress, it was like a scene from a pantomime and we couldn't help but be amused. Even though most of us were probably feeling pretty rotten, beds were shaking with laughter.

Eventually Mrs Doherty was transferred to a bed and then it was the turn of the nursing staff. They too had a difficult time. I felt sorry for Mrs Doherty, the world being such a dangerous place. Her bed was close to mine and, when she was finally on her own, I smiled at her and said soothingly, 'You will be all right now.'

I don't think she was soothed at all. Her response was short and to the point. Later that evening they moved her out of the ward and, as she was wheeled down the corridor, we could still hear her voice, insistent but growing fainter. I wonder where she is now. Go well, Mrs Doherty.

After Sue had phoned me, I went to bed and slept heavily.

Sunday 31st

I realise that I have woken myself up by singing 'Wichita Lineman' in my sleep.

Daughter Stevie arrives from Harrogate at eleven o'clock to take me to visit Sue. Stevie is very supportive, for which I'm grateful, though it makes me feel old and dependent. We stay with Sue for about an hour. I am more tired than I realised and I am glad to return home.

I spend the afternoon watching television. Nothing very challenging. I seem to remember somebody saying 'at this moment in time', the sort of phrase that begins by seeming clever, if rather pompous, and finally becomes irritating. Now only used by people who have too many words in their mouth.

Asleep by ten o'clock. New Year, like Christmas, comes and goes unobserved.

Monday 1st January
Spend the morning listening to a Christmas present CD, a compilation album by Jonas Kaufmann. Most people would say that compilation albums, particularly those made up of arias from different operas, are best listened to in part. However, because it's a present I feel an obligation to listen to the whole disc and by the end I'm suffering from aural exhaustion.

Whatever the circumstances, nothing could detract from this amazing voice, which so astonishes me that at the end of one aria I am shocked to tears. At one point a serene and seemingly effortless floating head note in Gounod's *Faust* is so singular that it reminds me of first hearing Jeff Buckley, some years ago, singing 'Hallelujah' (on *Private Passions*). Though it seems quite recent, I was on *Longfellow*, a Dutch barge, which must mean that it was at least twenty years ago.

Sue phones; she's waiting for medication and then she's coming home. Ruth and Amy are collecting her.

Memories
Childhood

The Wooden Chest

At the top of the house there was a wooden chest in an unoccupied attic room. It belonged to Uncle John. I never met him and I was told that he was the black sheep of the family. Because of this, I understood that he would never return to claim his property.

I cannot remember whether or not I was officially allowed to play with the contents of the chest, though Nana must have known what I was doing because I spent many hours up there.

For a small boy, long before political correctness or a responsible attitude to wildlife, the items in the chest represented treasure so exciting as to be almost beyond words.

The trunk contained a collection of birds' eggs, from the teeniest wren's egg to an enormous ostrich egg.

It contained a stamp collection with some unusually watermarked halfpenny greens which stood me in good stead at boarding school in later years.

It contained a butterfly collection.

It contained some pans of Winsor and Newton watercolours, new and bright, individually wrapped in waxed paper.

Finally, it contained three knives. The first was a Bowie knife with a solid black-onyx handle inlaid with a silver motif. The other two knives were a matched pair of North American Indian knives. They had long slim blades with a triangular cross-section, and the handles and the sheaths were decorated in coloured leather with bindings and tassels. I have always thought that these were skinning knives but, having just re-read Kurt Vonnegut's *Slaughterhouse Five,* I now think because of the shape of the blades that they might have been weapons.

I played with the knives for years. I cannot remember what happened to them. I raffled and swapped stamps from the collection throughout my time at secondary school but, more than seventy years later, what I really remember are the colours: the delicate blue of the thrush's egg, and the bright orange and yellow ochre of the little square tablets of watercolour paint. The fact that they had to be unwrapped before you could see the colour, rather like presents, made them seem very special.

Silver Glider

One summer when I was about nine or ten years old, I was staying at Nana's in Carlisle during my summer holidays. With the help of one of Nana's lodgers, I built a model glider aeroplane from a balsa-wood kit. The plane was covered in tissue paper which was then doped, causing it to shrink and tighten over the wooden framework. To my eyes, the finished plane looked very dull; although I knew that to paint it would increase its weight and affect its performance. I really wanted to paint it silver. My build companion (one of Nana's dispossessed lodgers), who was probably middle-aged, was just as excited as I was.

We bought a tin of silver dope at the model shop. Anyone who has used a cellulose dope or paint will know how strongly it smells. We used it indoors and the smell was overpowering; however, we didn't let a little thing like intoxication stop us.

When it was finished, the silver plane looked fantastic. We went down to a field by the river to test fly it. Unfortunately, the lift generated by the wings was unable to compete with the weight of paint and the plane dived into the ground.

Half a lifetime later I was walking through Carlisle centre, not having been back there since childhood. Suddenly a powerful smell of cellulose dope stopped me in my tracks. My companion could smell nothing. I was genuinely puzzled – and then I remembered the silver plane. At the same moment, I realised that I was close to the model shop. I looked around and recognised it. It was no longer a model shop but had the same frontage.

I know what a powerful stimulus smell can be. In this case, it seems that things were the wrong way round. A stimulus generated a smell which triggered a memory.

Joe and Me

Joe Shuttleworth was my friend throughout the time that I attended Glasshouses Primary School. He and I got up to all sorts of mischief, none of it particularly malicious but nearly all of it destined to get us into trouble.

In theory, I was not allowed to play with village boys. My father must have thought that we were superior to them in some way. This was an opinion that I didn't understand and therefore I didn't let it interfere with my activities. Whenever I could, I would leave home with a fishing rod, which was little more than a cane with a line and a bent pin on the end. I would walk along the road around the corner into the field where the stream ran, stash my rod in a hedge and head off down the bank to the village. Even then, I remember being amazed that my parents could be naïve enough to believe that a pretend fishing rod would keep me occupied until bedtime.

Joe was savvy in a way that I was not. Once, when we were walking through the woods together, I saw his father heading towards us. As he neared he asked, 'Have you seen our Joe?'

For a moment I was confused and then a sideways glance made me realise that I was on my own. 'No, Mr Shuttleworth.'

'When you see him, tell him I want him.'

'Yes, Mr Shuttleworth.'

I walked on. Fifty yards more and Joe slipped quietly out of the bushes; we fell into step and continued on our way.

We had a lot of fun. One evening Joe brought a hand axe from his home and we stopped at the Rope Mill's machine shop at the river's edge to have it sharpened. I'm sure that Joe said that his father had sent him with a request to sharpen the axe. We acquired a large ball of twine from somewhere, probably the mill, and we arrived at the riverbank with the intention of making a raft.

We cut down a number of saplings and, using the twine, we made a raft in the form of a lattice-work platform. After a lot of debate, I persuaded Joe to stand on the raft whilst I pushed him into the river. The whole thing was a complete failure. The raft sank almost immediately, leaving Joe standing in several feet of water.

On another occasion, Joe made me sit on the other side of the lane and watch whilst he climbed onto the low roof of his family cottage and pushed a sack down the chimney.

He joined me and we waited. I wasn't sure what to expect. A few minutes later, smoke began to billow out of the front door – followed quite quickly by Joe's grandma. I think that she was blind but she moved briskly. She knew exactly what had happened.

'Joe, you little bugger!' she shouted.

We were mischievous rather than malicious. We were children in a time that was very different to the present. No TV, no toys, few games. We were just a couple of boys with time on our hands. We had nothing to do other than the things we invented for ourselves.

As I look back, I'm ashamed that we cut down the saplings but I know that at the time we simply wanted to make a raft and it seemed the best way of doing it.

Our most public escapade was when we lit a small fire under a large wooden hut in a field behind some houses in the village. The hut was standing on a bank so that the side facing the field was elevated slightly above the ground. Hens had scratched out a sheltered cave between the supporting legs. Joe had the matches. We soon had a small fire going.

An adult, I forget who, came into the field and he was furious. He was shouting at the top of his voice and we ran away as fast as we could. 'Joe Shuttleworth, Robert McBurney, stop. I know who you are!'

Knowing that the game was up, I stopped. Joe, for whom the game was never up, kept on running.

Afterwards, I couldn't understand how so many adults could all be so angry about a small fire. It was quite disproportionate.

Fifty years later, when I remembered this episode and talked about it to my mother, she told me that the hut had contained an illegal store of petrol. On reflection, I can sympathise with all the adults who were involved. They must have been quite frightened about the potential repercussions if half of the village of Glasshouses had been blown up.

Sunny Bank Hall

For a peppercorn rent, my grandad (who I loved) and my grandma (who I loved less) lived most of their adult lives in part of Sunny Bank Hall.

Sunny Bank Hall is a timbered house set into the hillside overlooking the valley in Greetland. It was said to be the oldest house in the district. Seemingly there were no metal nails in its construction, only oak timbers and wooden pegs.

It was approached by walking over open ground from the road and then down some wide stone steps which led to the back of the house. The way to the front of the house was through a central passageway.

My grandparents occupied the front right-hand side of the house. The front door gave onto a large sitting room with an open fire. A teeny kitchen led off to the right. Behind this room a door led to the stairs and a stone-flagged back scullery.

Grandad was a lovely old man, smiling and gentle, with eyebrows like Denis Healey and large floppy ears which he could move by twitching his face. It seems that he was a bit of a devil in his youth but now he spent his days sitting by the fire, smoking and reading and drinking tea.

The mobile library brought him seven books a week, all thrillers. He would say that he had read most of them before, but he was happy enough to read them again.

On the few occasions that I stayed with them, he would tell me such fantastic bedtime stories that I couldn't sleep. His stories must have been a combination of the books that he was reading at the time. For example, suspended over Niagara Falls, Dracula and Dick Barton are locked in mortal combat whilst below hundreds of fearsome tribesmen shoot poisoned arrows at them.

My sister Mary remembers Grandad reading her a bedtime story where the final words were, 'So he took his sword and chopped off her head. Goodnight, see you in the morning.'

Grandma was a small, stout tyrant. Before retirement, she was a manager at a draper's in Elland. She was an active force in the local branch of the Business and Professional Women's Guild.

She disliked my mother. It seems that Grandma first met my mother on the platform at Halifax railway station. My mother and father got off the train arm in arm and my father's first words to his mother, by way of greeting, were, 'I don't like your hat, Ma.'

That my mother should have been present when her darling boy said this sealed my mother's fate.

I think that in Grandma's eyes, no one was good enough for her boy, whatever his shortcomings. As previously mentioned, he had been married to the daughter of a prominent Halifax family, who, in the early 1930s, had divorced him on the grounds of infidelity.

In the scullery, which was quite a large square room with a low ceiling, was a door that led down narrow steps to a priest hole. The hole was sealed with a log. It looked small to me, and I wondered how an adult could squeeze through it. I was told that there was a documented tunnel that led up to the church; I longed to investigate but it was forbidden.

I knew that other families lived in the hall but I never saw any of them. Walking through the central passageway, there were doors to left and right which were never open.

One summer day, in the middle of the afternoon, the door to the right was open. Initially I was attracted by the noise. There was shouting and laughter and I saw a number of people. The detail I particularly remember is of a central figure, a big man in uniform, sitting on a bench at a table and banging a tankard down hard on its surface whilst talking to a woman who was leaning over him. I clearly remember feeling a sense of embarrassment. I felt as if I was spying on a private adult party.

I went into the house and told Grandad what I had seen, that I had seen into that part of the house that was at the back. Grandad couldn't understand what I was talking about, so we went out into the passage and I showed him the door.

He took me back into the scullery and, opening the inner door to a lean-to coal house, showed me the door on the outer wall a few feet beyond which led into the passageway.

Seventy years later I have no doubt about what I saw: a noisy group of adults, drinking, flirting, enjoying themselves, maybe from the seventeenth century but definitely there on that day in the 1940s.

The Duck

My first experience of fly-fishing was as a boy of ten or eleven years of age. A friend of my mother who lived in Wetheral – I remember him only as Alec – introduced me to the techniques of 'tackling up'. An important part of this was how to tie lengths of nylon together using a blood knot. I stood on his lawn one spring evening and tied this knot time and time again until he was confident that it was perfect.

That night he and a friend took me to fish a small lake that was very shallow and full of little trout. It was a warm dark night and I stood in the lake in my wellingtons and cast as best I could, with little idea as to where my fly was landing.

I fished without success for some time and then, from somewhere in front of me, I felt a strong tug on the line. Almost immediately the line went slack and, feeling no resistance, I thought that I had lost what I assumed to be a big trout. A second or two later, very surprisingly, I felt an even bigger tug from behind me. Even more strange, the tug felt as if it was coming from above head height. It took a moment or two, and the sound of beating wings, for me to realise that I had hooked a flying bird.

Alec came to my aid. We reeled the duck in gently (for that's what it was) and he released it without harm. I don't think I caught a trout that night but the magic of fly-fishing took its hold on me.

In my case, I think that the scenery and the beauty of the river have been more important to me than catching fish. More often than not I have fished alone; nights spent sea-trout fishing, with every fibre of one's being alive to the excitement of one's surroundings, have left indelible memories.

I have not fished for five years, partly through laziness and partly because I have found it increasingly difficult to reconcile my pleasure with the catching of a wild animal. And yet I have no argument with the millions of people who fish and enjoy every moment of it. I have been one of their number for most of my life.

Maybe my feelings are just one aspect of growing older, so I may yet tie a couple more blood knots and spend a glorious day knee-deep in the peaty, rocky waters of the Yorkshire Dales.

Eleven Plus

I was a pupil at Glasshouses Primary School when I sat my eleven-plus examination in Pateley Bridge. I remember a large room with rows and rows of desks, and I remember an early instruction on the exam paper which was to write G for a girl or a B for a boy in the blank circle at the top of the paper.

An adult supervisor, walking up and down the rows and peering at the papers, tapped on mine. I looked up and saw an amused but querulous expression on her face. Then I realised that I had accidentally put G in my circle. I was very embarrassed and hoped that she wouldn't tell anybody else about it. I remember nothing else about the paper.

Sometime later the letter came to say that I passed the examination, and I imagine it said that I had a place at Ripon Grammar School.

Miss Knight was the head teacher at Glasshouses Primary School. I believe that I was the first of her pupils who had ever passed the eleven plus. She was very pleased with me and she gave me half a crown. By invitation, my mother and I walked down to her cottage in the village to receive it. Miss Knight was a formidable single lady. Having only ever seen her in school, I was amazed to realise that she lived in a normal house, surrounded by normal furniture. Up to that point, I don't think I had ever thought of her as having a life outside the classroom.

Diary

2nd January– 26th January 2018

January 2018

Tuesday 2nd

A quiet day. Callers with soups and flowers. Both of us very tired. I watch TV.

I am back on my high horse about the way that we use the word 'save'. Quite knowingly we use it not to indicate saving but to indicate spending, with the assumption that we are spending less than we might otherwise have done. We price things to ninety-nine pence, knowing full well that a penny change is not going to be significant; despite this, both the seller and the buyer draw comfort from the arrangement.

Have we reached a point where, in general terms, we mistrust anyone who is too straightforward, who doesn't make the effort to sell to us by pulling the wool over our eyes? Could it be that we feel the same way about our politicians? Was truth always so difficult to deal with?

Wednesday 3rd

On the BBC news page website there is an article about a dating agency having to withdraw a poster from the London Underground because it suggested that scientific methods were being used in its selection process.

Just before Christmas, Sue attended a funeral service. It was the funeral of an old and much-loved man who had been a resident in the care home where Sue's mother lives. It seems that Jim – that is what we shall call him – was a convert to a born-again church. In his address, the preacher explained that Jim had embraced this faith as a result of the most rigorous and scientific personal research. The preacher went on to say that, given his belief in God, Jim would certainly be reunited with his loved ones. However, he then threatened the non-believers in the congregation with the knowledge that on their death they would have an individual interview with an angry God.

These threats of violence were quite startling. As a nominal Christian, now an agnostic, and having been brought up with the idea that God is supposed to be all-forgiving, I was surprised to hear of this. I wondered if it was a reflection of violent modern times. Whatever the rights and wrongs of it all, I always think that Christians should feel sympathy for those people of different cultures and geography who know nothing about Christianity. If the path to redemption is as narrow as the preacher suggested, it does seem rather unfair on them. Let us hope that they feel equal sympathy for us.

Thursday 4th

Every second advertisement on the sports channel seems to be about gambling. Gamblers and would-be gamblers are encouraged to believe that they are players in the thick of the action. The idea of them taking control is sold heavily. At the end of each advertisement there is usually the sad little line which says: 'When the fun stops, stop.'

Having seen the faces of people, usually men, in bookies, and having known gamblers (my father as a younger man, his friends, my friends), fun might seem to be the last word one would use to describe their involvement.

As a young boy I remember being taken to a racecourse with my father and two or three of his friends. It would have been Ripon or Doncaster or maybe York. There was a tipster called Prince Honolulu, who impressed me enormously. He was brilliantly dressed in coloured silks, tall and black, with plumes in his headdress. He shouted, 'I gotta horse, I gotta horse.'

My father must have bought a tip from him because I remember the horse was called Keepatwoatwo and it won.

However, on the journey back home that evening, one of my father's friends, sitting on the floor in the back of the van, was very quiet. Occasionally he sang sentimental songs in a rather lovely voice. My father whispered to me that he had had a 'bad day'. Years later I learned that he had eventually gambled away the farm that he had inherited, and was employed as an agricultural labourer by the new owner.

Our Border Terrier, Ruby, came back today. I think that she's had a wonderful time in Harrogate. She has shared the house with a two-year-old black Labrador called Derek. It seems that she flirted with Derek to a point where he was so confused that he tried to hide. Even then she would not leave him alone, trying to seduce him with her pink pig. If only a pink pig would do it for us all.

Friday 5th
As I go to bed, Sue is watching a Beatles programme. I'm not sure if it's a tribute or genuine footage. It brings back memories of standing on the runway at Manchester with my then-wife Jackie, next to the plane that was taking me to Germany in my role as lieutenant, National Service, Royal Army Service Corps. It was probably early to mid-sixties. In those days families and friends wandered

out to the plane and said goodbye at the foot of the aircraft steps. At the other end of the plane, four young men were saying goodbye to their individual girlfriends. I remember asking Jackie if she knew who they were and telling her, 'It's that new group, The Beatles.'

There were very few of us on the plane and I never saw them again. I think they were going to one of their first gigs in Germany and it might have been one of the last times in their lives when they had some privacy in a public place. I guess that it was the last time that they were seen off by only four girls.

I also remember that at the end of the flight I had a military form to complete as 'Officer i/c Flight', even though it was a conventional commercial aircraft. As with many military forms, one was careful to provide answers that would not complicate issues. The steward on the plane told me hair-raising tales about planes having landed with a cupful of fuel left in the tank. However, he was quick to assure me that no such thing had happened on our flight. I think that he also chose to avoid any complications in my answers that might have returned to bite him.

Saturday 6th

Neighbour Diane takes Ruby and her spaniel, also called Ruby, for a long walk through the woods. They return more than an hour and a half later with the dogs covered in mud. Thank goodness for a large-pan sink, a small dog and a lovely neighbour.

I spend most of the day using voice to text on Speech Texter which I then cut and paste and save on LibreOffice Writer.

After six hours, exhausted but quite pleased with myself, I find that I have lost all but the last part of my work. I suspect that I failed to save it correctly or overwrote it with something else. Prior to my recent efforts to drag myself into the present day, I was a Luddite. Now I wonder if I've done the right thing by trying to change. It's pen and ink versus the computer. Rather like the tortoise and the hare.

Sunday 7th

I spend part of the day looking for my lost copy. I have to believe that somehow, if I can only find the correct button to press, my hours of work will pop up on the screen. 'We were just hiding,' the words will say. I will laugh (I suspect that it will be a hollow laugh) and I will press the print button and make solemn promises to myself that THIS WILL NEVER HAPPEN AGAIN!

In the late afternoon I begin to rewrite. Fortunately it is easier than I had imagined, probably because things are fresh in my mind. Sometimes Speech Texter is surprisingly accurate and then it fails, joining words together, giving me capitals for no apparent reason and occasionally giving me quite creative alternatives to the words spoken, such as 'last coffee' for 'lost copy'.

Monday 8th

Late last night, a car slid on the ice and crashed into the lamp post outside our garden. I saw the hazard lights flashing as I came around the corner with Ruby during her bedtime walk. A couple of neighbours had come out and were standing with the driver, who understandably looked disconsolate. He was quite a young man, and I imagine the last thing he wanted so soon after Christmas was the expense of having his car towed away and repaired. The nearside front wheel was pushed up into the wing, and it looked as if he would need a suspended tow.

I walked through the woods with Ruby this morning. This was my first real outing since my illness. I went with Diane and Peter. We saw a beautiful, large, dark-coloured fox in the big wood. Fortunately, neither of the dogs saw it. I think that my Ruby would be unstoppable if she saw a fox, and I dread to think what might happen if she faced up to an animal half as big again as she is.

Ruby has her work cut out trying to catch squirrels. This has been an obsession of hers for most of her five years. 'Squirrel' is one of the few words that she recognises. She used to be faster across the ground than a squirrel but she lacked the cunning to catch one. Now she may have more cunning (which I doubt) but she's also put on a little bit of weight, which has slowed her down. I think the squirrels just have the edge. They are very clever; they run past a tree, turn sharply and climb. At this point Ruby usually thunders on, wondering where they've gone.

Tuesday 9th

I was in Malaga before Christmas. An article in an English-language version of a local paper bemoaned the fact that punishments for people convicted of serious cruelty to animals are inadequate. The writer, who I think was a senior legal figure, went on to explain that Spanish attitudes towards animals are changing with a new generation; whereas previously, animals were traditionally regarded merely as property, it is now accepted that they are sentient beings and that the law should change to reflect this.

Last week I watched a TV programme about the Spanish Armada in which it was explained that, having travelled north on the English coast, the ships, which had not been provisioned for such a long voyage, began to run out of food and water. As a result, horses and mules were driven into the sea where they had no hope of survival.

I thought that this was unbearable. With my head full of guilt, I suddenly remembered that British sea captains threw many living black slaves into the sea because Lloyds of London would pay out insurance for a drowned slave but not for one who had died naturally.

Wednesday 10th

I have spent much of the day thinking about the things I wrote yesterday. We have inherited a past which, in part, is deeply shameful, and we live in a present which is violent and frightening. Genocide, war crimes and dying children are our daily diet of television news. Possibly it was always like this, but we are better informed because of more sophisticated communications. Even so, I imagine that I am like so many others in that I feel pessimistic and helpless in the face of so much violence and intolerance. I remember that at the Millennium many people said surely this is an opportunity for us to create a peaceful world! How misplaced our hopes have become.

In my own case, I would go out of my way to avoid direct confrontation with anyone who was overtly racist or fascist or violent, even though I recognise that my inaction creates a vacuum in which others, behaving in a way that I deplore, can flourish.

I know that there are millions of people like me who wish that they had the courage to contribute in a meaningful way to society and are full of admiration for those that do. We are what used to be described as the silent majority. Sue says that most people do the best that that they can most of the time, and there is comfort to be had from that thought. We can't put the world to rights; maybe the best that we can do is to accept responsibility for our own behaviour on a day-to-day basis.

Thursday 11th

I live in Horsforth. Before it became a district of Leeds, it was known as the largest village in England. On the few occasions I've heard Horsforth referred to by the BBC, they have pronounced the name in full. Most people who live here, with or without a Leeds accent, call it 'Horsfuth'.

Isn't pronunciation important? I once spent quite a long time in a New York City deli trying to buy some butter. Admittedly the proprietor was Korean but he spoke with a proud New York accent. I gesticulated, mimed and pointed, but it was only when he said 'Burrer' that we both knew what we were talking about.

Friday 12th

Walked with Diane and the two Rubys through the woods this morning. Diane told me a wonderful story.

When she was about eight or nine years old, she had a friend whose father was a representative for Thackeray's medical company. He travelled the world demonstrating their equipment by means of a Betamax tape, which he played on a portable screen. One of the procedures, which was demonstrated in full, was a hip replacement. It seems that this tape was played at her friend's birthday party. Diane tells me that on first viewing, as the scalpel made the initial cut, all the girls screamed in horror. However, they quickly got over the shock and enjoyed the film so much that it became a great favourite and no future party was complete without it.

Saturday 13th

I have spent the day packing because I am going to France on Monday. I am going for a week to spend time with my son, Marcus, who lives in Perpignan. I am slightly anxious about the journey.

I catch a train from Leeds to Manchester airport and then I fly to Carcassonne with Ryanair. The last time I flew to Carcassonne with Ryanair, the return flight was cancelled the night before. Seemingly it was to do with French air traffic control operators who had called a strike. Whatever the reason, it left us in an impossible situation where we had to arrange an alternative flight back, in this case from Spain.

Fingers crossed. Hopefully Marcus will remember to meet me at Carcassonne, which is about an hour and a half away from Perpignan. Of course he will – I'm just being like fathers with their sons the world over.

Marcus telephoned me to tell me that a friend of his called Christian was on his way back from Toulouse and would pick me up at the airport. I asked him if I knew Christian and he said, 'No.'

'How will he recognise me?'

'I told him that you looked like Sean Connery, not as he looked when he was playing James Bond, of course, but as he looks now.'

Poor Sean Connery, I thought, if it's come to this.

Monday 15th

Travelling to France. Leave home at ten to eight. I always like to be ridiculously early. We joke that I would really like to be in a hotel next to the runway the night before. As it is, I catch an earlier train into Leeds and an earlier train to Manchester airport, where I arrive an hour and a quarter before check-in opens.

The view from the train is particularly grim in the blue-grey half-light of a wet morning. I wouldn't like to think that it was anyone's abiding memory of the cross-Pennine industrial belt. The sad scenery belies the fact that the people here are generally warm-hearted. They smile at you, they talk to you, they help each other. All this nonsense about a Yorkshireman being dour and mean, like a Scotsman with the generosity washed off – rubbish! Largesse everywhere. Actually, that might be a bit of an exaggeration; on reflection, it could even cause offence.

Finding the whole experience of sitting in the airport lounge quite surreal. The noise level is high and quite metallic because of all the hard surfaces. Few people seem completely relaxed. They sit and watch their phones or tablets or the big screen. Time hangs. The overriding sensation is one of transience, as indeed one would expect. It takes its toll on me. I'm not a good traveller.

In the plane twenty minutes after take-off, gleaming white clouds rolling to the horizon, brilliant sun, pale blue sky. It still surprises that every day is sunny and bright above cloud level.

Arrive at Carcassonne about four-thirty European time. Three hours to wait for my lift. Unfortunately, at five-thirty the airport closes, except for one entrance porch, unlit, with a small metal bench where staff wait for their lifts. Eventually that too closes, and I spend some time walking up and down the pavements wheeling my case and trying to stay warm.

Christian and Thomas arrive on time. The car is warm and I have animated conversation with Thomas, mainly political, both of us anxious about Brexit.

I arrive at Marcus's house about nine o'clock. A warm greeting from him and my granddaughter, Chloe, who is nine. She brings me drawings and small gifts. I wish I had known she would be there, I would have brought something for her with me. As it is, she carefully watches me unpack my case, I think in hope.

I have arranged to take her and her mum shopping for a late Christmas present during the week. I don't know if she is aware of this.

Tuesday 16th
Up late. Marcus has gone to work and taken Chloe to school on the way. He will be home by six o'clock. Chloe will be collected from school by her mother, Florence, and taken swimming. Back here by seven o'clock.

I find a note from Marcus about shops and routes and a final note saying the key is in the door. I misread this and I think that it says the key is *on* the door. I try to find it on the sliding patio doors to the front of the room, without success. It seems to me that if I cannot lock the door, I will have to stay in the house until Marcus returns. I search for food and find a small amount of bread and a jar of jam which I think will have to last me until the evening.

Marcus has two dogs, a boxer dog called Diamond and a black-and-white mongrel bitch called Maya. Normally they live and sleep in the garden where they have a kennel. They are allowed in the house because I am there. They are very affectionate and obviously thrilled to be inside because they take up residence on the sofa, curl up together and sleep.

I am making a pencil drawing of Diamond, who is asleep, when Maya steals my Artgum eraser. She trots out into the garden, wagging her tail with pleasure, and tries to keep away from me while she investigates her prize. I remember puppy training rules and break off a piece of my precious bread to make an exchange. She is very pleased with this, and leaves me with the feeling that I might have encouraged her to steal other things. Just in case, I put everything out of reach.

I draw and photograph the dogs for a few hours. After lunch (tea and bread) I find a book that I think I gave to Marcus about twenty-five years ago, *Watercolors and Drawings of the French Impressionists* by Horst Keller, translated from the German and published in New York in 1982. I rush through it to find the image that made such a strong impression on me all those years ago, Paul

Signac's *View of the Seine in Paris*. In searching for it, I find Edouard Vuillard's *Breakfast in the Country*. Pastel on coloured paper. It is so beautiful. The blue of the dress next to blues, pinks and mauves tugs at one's heart. I just want to rush off and make marks with pastels.

My drawings of the dogs are merely outlines with no attempt at creating volume. For the moment I am learning their faces. Unfortunately, they are on constant alert for anyone passing on the road, so they leap out of the drawing suddenly and often.

This house has several of my drawings from twenty years ago. Seeing them again, I'm quite impressed and quite depressed because I think I'm going backwards!

In the late afternoon I do a big shop with Florence, Marcus's ex, a beautiful woman whom I miss as a daughter-in-law.

Wednesday 17th
A day with Chloe. Good breakfast, Marcus delightfully attentive and affectionate. The day with Chloe begins with Play-Doh and cartoons on TV. Thank goodness for TV and, in this case, Walt Disney. The sheer creative inventiveness of children's cartoons is amazing.

I read that Trump's doctors have stated that his cognitive abilities are fully normal. This is, if one accepts it, a disappointment. His pronouncements have been so inappropriate that one has taken comfort in the idea that he might not be entirely to blame for them, that some impairment might mitigate in his favour. It seems not to be so. Even so, and despite what seems to me to be an appalling record, one can almost feel sorry for him. To be goaded and mocked – is this what he wanted? The wrong bull in the wrong china shop.

I talk to Sue. Snow, gales and sleet at home in England. Blue sky and white clouds here, but windy and not warm.

Thursday 18th

Marcus takes Chloe to school and returns unexpectedly to say that a Range Rover has reversed into his car, damaging the bonnet. It was a slow-speed collision. It seems that the parking alarm sounded in the Range Rover, but the driver mistook it for the front alarm whilst Marcus, seeing what was about to happen, pressed desperately on the centre of his steering wheel, forgetting that the horn pad was at the edges of the boss. Technology! Meant to serve, not to confuse.

I have found the key and realised that it belongs to the back door, but I am unable to close the faulty door lock so I have decided to stay and write and draw. I draw the draped tablecloth and the table legs. A simple enough subject, but drawing fabric is usually a challenge. On the positive side, it doesn't leap about like dogs.

Friday 19th

A revelatory article about Trump by Tony Schwartz in the *Guardian* today. I think that Schwartz was the co-author of the 'Art of the Deal' with Trump some years ago. He talks about one side of Trump being the frightened child of a relentlessly critical and bullying father and a distant and disengaged mother who couldn't – or wouldn't – protect him. As is often said, the child is father of the man.

Last evening, I went shopping for Chloe's Christmas present with Florence then back to Marcus's for a supper of salad and soup and cake.

Lucas, who is living in Marcus's flat next door, joined us for supper. He and Marcus opened a bottle of Steinraffler Lagrein from 2001. The cork was so difficult to pull that Marcus had to take the bottle outside and hammer it inwards until it moved a fraction, after which he was able to draw it. The wine was a beautiful tawny colour.

It is possibly seven or eight years since I tasted alcohol. I smelled the bouquet of this wine, which was delicious, but happily I felt no desire to taste it. When I do think about wine, I remember a sunny grassy bank in France, the incredible smell and taste of warm tomatoes, crusty bread and chilled wine. I choose not to think of the many stupid befuddled episodes which unfortunately outnumber the enjoyable ones.

Saturday 20th
I finally managed the door lock and had quite a long walk. I passed the Mas des Fleurs, which offers accommodation. On my return I looked it up, and was amused to see that it offers beautiful views across the lettuce fields of Jardins St Jaques. Coming from the North of England, the idea

of a lettuce field is almost surreal. It occurs to me that the 'lettuce fields of St Jacques' almost rhymes with the 'liquorice fields of Pontefract'.

I dreamt about the photographic darkroom last night. It is a recurrent dream that I have not visited for some time. The darkroom appears to be underground and is approached through long, arched, rough-hewn tunnels. The first tunnel, the largest, is featureless but the smaller tunnels, still arched, which branch off the end of it like fingers on a hand, are lined with recessed doors. The doors are unmarked; in my dreams, I'm always surprised that I'm able to find the correct one despite it being some distance along the row. Last night I feared that the room, which I think of as secret and abandoned by its original owners, might have been destroyed. I found the room but did not enter it.

This darkroom is unlike any of the professional darkrooms with which I've been involved. It is larger – made up of two rooms – and complex. I wonder if it has its genesis in a military establishment that I might have seen, possibly as a child, but which I can no longer remember. Possibly my father took me once to the aircraft works at Yeadon. I wish I knew.

Once, on manoeuvres in Germany, my platoon stayed in a camp of low wooden buildings, long deserted, which we were told had been the headquarters of the Hitler Youth. It seems that at a later date the camp was used for displaced persons. We explored the spaces above the rooms under the eaves. They were full of old suitcases and personal ephemera covered in dust. We didn't touch anything – we didn't dare. It was all rather unnerving.

Outside, in the middle of the camp, there was an entrance to an underground shelter. It was a long earthen tunnel that sloped down into the ground. We took torches to explore it, but the roof had collapsed some distance in. Though we could have climbed over the fallen earth, for safety reasons we chose not to go further. We shone the torches around but could see nothing other than the tunnel disappearing into darkness. I suppose it is of such things that dreams are made.

I have always been nervous about being underground in much the same way that I suffer badly from vertigo. Strangely enough, I could hang out of a helicopter when working with a camera in my hand but I have to be dragged onto a balcony in a holiday hotel.

Marcus is at work. Chloe is watching TV. The stove is happily consuming huge logs.

Sunday 21st

Another unusual dream in which I enter hospital voluntarily to self-treat some skin ailment on my neck and shoulders. The bed is too large and someone arranges for it to be divided into two. Then for some reason I too have to be divided. A doctor suggests that he could be divided on my behalf. I think he's rather noble to suggest this but I recognise that it's my problem and that I really have to subject myself to the process.

A nurse puts a blunt-ended scissor blade up my right nostril and begins to cut. The experience is horribly realistic. I feel no pain but, knowing suddenly that I cannot go through with it, I panic and wake, shaking violently.

Marcus tells me that I can find the meaning of dreams on Google. I haven't looked. I'm sure that's wise.

Monday 22nd

Up early to say goodbye to Chloe. Marcus decides on an early trip to the airport. Better safe than sorry in his little car, which is only 660cc. We have a job to push my large suitcase into the boot.

We arrive early in Carcassonne and drive down to the harbour to see where our boat *Juno* used to be moored. Parking is impossible, so rather than eating by the harbour we go to the airport café. We arrive about 1pm, which is three and a half hours before my flight.

During the journey in the car, which takes an hour and a half, we talk and laugh. Marcus tells me a story of the Frenchman who, owing €1103 to the revenue, reads about €1100 toilet seats in the Lycée Palace. Understandably incensed, and by way of protest, he sends three euros and a Brico Depot toilet seat to the authorities. Altogether we have a good bonding journey, never fast, but we have lots of time.

My flight back from France was uneventful. I arrived at Manchester airport railway station at about 6.15. The first train back to Leeds was the York train at 7.24. I waited on platform 3B, which at that time on a January evening was surprisingly inhospitable.

Then began a series of texts about a fish pie: Sue wanted to know when I would arrive in Leeds and when she should put the pie in the oven. I tried to do the calculations, but my final suggestion was to wait until I was nearly in Leeds when I would send a text. I said that I would catch a taxi. Text followed text. Somehow the subject of the fish pie assumed a disproportionate significance.

We have a private joke. Some years ago, a landscape gardener we knew would start rubbing his hands together at about quarter to five and say, 'I wonder what pie our lass'll put in the microwave tonight.' I knew that Sue's texts referred to this. However, I was tired and my texts were short and to the point.

We pulled into Leeds. I caught a taxi and was home fifteen minutes later. I was very pleased to be there, and Sue was pleased to see me after a week away. I was really too tired to eat and, though I made an effort, I could only manage a very small piece of pie.

Tuesday 23rd

First day back from France. Ruby was ecstatic last night. We walk in the woods, Ruby swims in the stream. Flowers and chocs for our neighbour Diane who has walked Ruby in my absence. Peter calls for coffee and chat and tells me a nice story about his father during the Second World War.

Seemingly Peter's father volunteered at the beginning of the war. He was commissioned and given the job of erecting more than two hundred searchlights on the west coast between Devon and the north of Scotland. At some point during this project, his detachment received a typewriter that was packaged in a crate. Once the crate was removed, the packaging was found to be chopped up petrol coupons. Petrol was rationed and petrol coupons were precious. Over a period of months, the coupons were painstakingly reassembled, using gummed paper which was designed for repairing sheet music. (Sellotape had not been invented.)

Peter tells me that his father's detachment had a strict set of rules for using these petrol coupons. For some reason they were not to be used in Yorkshire; presumably one of the principals lived there. They were not to be used anywhere near where the detachment was currently stationed. The way in which they were used was that one person would remain in the vehicle with the engine running whilst the second person paid for the fuel then handed in the coupons before running back to the vehicle and making a getaway.

Interestingly, Peter's father ran an SS90 Jaguar to the amazement of his commanding officer who ran an Austin Seven.

Wednesday 24th

Walking with Ruby this morning, Peter and I have a politically incorrect conversation. It concerns the sort of partners which we might have in the distant future. I'm not sure if we're thinking about humanoids like Dolly the sheep or automata; we don't go into detail. We discuss the specification which we might ask for when we place our order. Peter would like somebody or something which looks like Rachel Weisz. Peter is very knowledgeable about all things mechanical. He rebuilds cars. I suggest that part of Peter's order might include a request for a software download of the complete Hayne's motor repair manuals. Peter thinks this is a great idea.

'Well,' he says, 'at least we would be able to have a meaningful conversation.'

January 26th 2018

Sue and I take Sue's mum to Otley hospital for minor surgery on her lower eyelid.

Whilst we are waiting, the TV programme is featuring a prize-winning fish and chip outlet. Though I don't hear it, Sue tells me that mushy peas are described as 'Yorkshire Caviar'.

Memories
School and First Job

Ripon Grammar School

At school we had a small outdoor pool. Every morning we had a choice: swim or run. I hated running but I couldn't swim. However, because the pool was small I was able to do a fast racing dive, a couple of crawl strokes and reach the other side – but that was my limit.

In our physics lesson we were told that the specific gravity of the human body is less than that of water. This impressed me because, as a non-swimmer, I needed something positive in which to believe. I really wanted to swim.

I was in the Combined Cadet Force and one afternoon we had an RAF survival team who demonstrated some aspect of training with rubber dinghies in the swimming pool.

I sat in a dinghy and, when it was in the middle of the deepest section of the pool, I rolled backwards over the edge. I went straight to the bottom and then kicked off and up to the surface, where I was able to take a breath before sinking again. I tried to angle my jumps towards the edge and not panic, but progress was very slow and it took an extraordinary number of attempts before I reached safety. I was too exhausted to pull myself out of the pool and surprised that no one else had noticed my difficulty. I think that I was probably about twelve years old. I was very thin; thinking about it later, it occurred to me that my specific gravity might not have been quite as advantageous as it would be to other, plumper boys.

When I was fourteen, I was at home in Bradford for the summer holidays. Holidays were not much fun. I had lived in so many places and I was away at school; because of this I didn't know anyone in Bradford of my own age.

I decided to go swimming in Drummond Road Baths. This was a walk from my home near Lister Park. Part of me still believed, with a sort of fatalism, in the specific gravity theory. This suggested that, even if I did nothing, I would survive.

The baths were very old-fashioned, even for the fifties. Curtained cubicles down each side gave straight onto the edge of the pool. I changed into my swimming trunks – I think that they were knitted wool. Because I was so thin, the short legs flapped around my thighs and I was very aware that from any angle below knee-height I was exposed to view.

To avoid being embarrassed, I threw open the curtain of my cubicle, ran and jumped far out into the water in one fluid movement. I was surprised at how deep it was. I swallowed a lot of water.

As I surfaced, probably for the second time and realising that I was in trouble, I grabbed a figure in front of me who happened to be a well-built girl of about my own age. I held onto her bust – or at least the fabric which contained her bust. At first, she laughed good-naturedly and, bringing her arms up inside mine, tried to knock my hands away. Unable to let go, I tried to explain to her that this was not a game, that I was drowning and I needed help. However, water gushed out of my mouth rather than words. Possibly she mistook the desperate appeal in my eyes for malice because she began to scream.

The attendant blew a whistle and my partner, to whom I was now locked, struggled to the edge of the pool taking me with her. By this time most of the girls in the baths were screaming. I hadn't realised that one side was for the boys and the other side was for the girls. As we got out of the water on the girls' side the attendant probably thought that a fairly serious situation might be developing. She shouted, 'Girls' side, girls' side.'

I disengaged myself and ran around the edge of the pool as fast as I could, back to my cubicle and safety, where I dressed and left in record time. So much for swimming.

Cadet Camp

I was in the RAF Cadets at school. One summer, I think in 1952, we went for a summer camp to RAF St Mawgan in Cornwall.

We travelled by train. I am unsure of our station of departure. Probably York or Leeds. I know that we changed at Crewe.

Collectively, we were no more horrid than any group of thirteen-year-old boys let off the leash could be.

Before the train pulled away from the station, we sat as far back in our window seats as possible. Reaching forward with one hand, we took turns in holding open copies of the magazine *Health and Efficiency* against the glass.

Health and Efficiency was the naughtiest magazine then in normal circulation. It was full of nude photographs of men and women strategically posed and airbrushed. Even at that time it was woefully old-fashioned.

People on the platform came forward to peer at what must have looked like railway notices in the corners of the train windows. Several ladies recoiled in shock. We were delighted and thought it hilariously funny in the way that only smutty thirteen-year-old boys can feel.

In Crewe, I stole cigarettes from the newsagents on the platform. I know that lots of kids have pinched things, but I am ashamed. I have regretted this all of my adult life. I don't think that I have ever been back to Crewe but I've always thought that if I did so, I should replace the cigarettes. It is probably too late now and the newsagent is probably long gone. In truth, I've only mentioned this in case someone who was there with me should read this and 'dob' on me!

When we arrived at the camp, we were billeted in large bell tents. We ate in the main dining hall with the men. It all seemed very grown-up.

Cornwall was glorious. Most of us had never been in the south of England before, and the closeness of the landscape and the colours of the earth were a revelation.

We spent one sunlit day lazing around on the grass next to a runway whilst waiting our turn to be taken for a flight in a Tiger Moth. Two volunteer ladies ran a little wooden cabin next to the runway where we could buy drinks and snacks. They sold a fruit juice that was unlike anything that we knew. Today we would probably call it a smoothie; it was sweet and cold and the flavour was incredibly intense. The day was hot and we were exposed. We drank this wonderful sweet juice one slow sip after another, making it last for as long as possible until we ran out of money.

I think that not much had changed at St Mawgan since the end of the war. I can imagine RAF pilots lounging near that hut waiting for a scramble.

When my turn for a flight came, the pilot, who was a Wing Commander (long scarf and all the kit), asked me what I would like to do. I was quite excited and I said, 'Everything please.' I think that he was getting bored with all the 'circuits and bumps', and he was obviously pleased with this response. He explained to me that the plane could do the complete stunt pattern except for an outside loop, technically called a bunt.

The flight was exciting – loops, rolls, stall turns. I remember the sense of weightlessness when the earth seemed to spin around me and I looked up at the ground whilst floating above my seat. In reality, of course, I was upside down at the top of a loop.

I longed to be a pilot but I wore glasses so I knew that it could never happen. Years later, when I was conscripted and given a choice of three services, I chose the Army. I couldn't swim so I was a bit scared of the Navy; I couldn't choose the RAF because that would have meant that I stayed on the ground whilst others flew, the thought of which I couldn't bear.

One day, we went out on an RAF launch. The skipper poked his head out of the wheelhouse and said that the conditions were choppy. We could stay on deck if we wished but, having made that decision, we would have to be outside for the whole of the trip as he was going to close the hatches.

Naturally enough, at thirteen we were all 'man enough' to laugh at the elements.

One of my friends stood on the foredeck with one arm nonchalantly around a mast whilst holding a cheap briar pipe in the other hand, occasionally taking a puff. He looked very cool. He was sick halfway across the bay. I was aft and alerted to this by the sight of a large amount of vomit flashing past me at eye level. It had formed a pleasing shape in the air, rather like a misshapen pizza.

We had one day off duty, it was probably the Sunday. We were told that if we left the aerodrome by the 'back gate', we could walk the few miles into Newquay. Three or four of us set off. It was a baking hot day. Trapped between high hedges on small roads, the walk seemed to last forever.

At one point we passed a little farmyard with an old man and a bull. The old man was tiny and wizened, like someone that Arthur Rackham might have painted. The bull was old. It had misshapen feet and seemed to be balancing on tiptoes. The old man loved the bull. He stroked it and talked to it. He told us that he and the bull had grown old together and, though there wasn't much future for either of them, he was not unhappy.

This has become an abiding memory for me. It was probably the first time that we, as young teenagers, had been taken into the confidence of an adult – a stranger – on matters as significant as ageing and death; that we had been treated as equals.

Newquay seemed beautiful on that glorious day. Before we set off back to camp, we watched the sun, red like a blood orange, sink into the sea.

On one of our last days, some of us were fortunate enough to go on a simulated bombing exercise in Lancaster bombers. Despite its size, the inside of a Lancaster bomber offers very little comfort. Moving through the plane is a series of squeezes and sharp turns between steel lockers and corners.

We flew over the Atlantic for a couple of hours and then dropped simulated bombs, which I was told were pieces of silver paper. On the return leg, I crawled under the pilot's seat to reach the front of the nose cone. As I remember it, the whole of the underside of the nose cone was made up of glass blocks set in a metal lattice-work frame. This gives the occupier an amazing view, 360 degrees, whilst feeling as if one is hanging in space.

I stayed in the nose cone for much of the return trip, watching the panorama of the sea beneath me. As we approached the land the sea changed colour, not gradually as one might expect, but sometimes quite sharply as if reflecting changes in the seabed. From deep blue-black, it changed through the blues until it became a bright cerulean before giving way to the light gold of the beach. I could see the people clearly though they seemed very small. It was all so new; it was enchanting.

Waiting for Benskin

Most schools have an annual speech day and Ripon Grammar School was no exception. The speech day was held in 'Big School' and probably bored the parents as much as it bored the boys.

The usual endless speeches were interspersed with various prizes, often quite unsuitable. In my case, I was presented one year with the Middle School Memorial Divinity Prize. I'm still not sure how or why that happened. It would be even less appropriate now.

That same year, the speech day experience was enlivened for us all – that is for all of the boys – because the parents and staff knew nothing of what was to happen.

A boy called Benskin was scheduled to recite a monologue in Greek. I think that Benskin was in the sixth form. He was unknown to me at the time. The majority of us had no idea that Greek was being taught in the school. Artie Shaw was our Latin teacher, and we guessed that he must have been doing one-off tutoring for Benskin, as Greek was not on the curriculum.

The news, which swept through the school like wildfire, was that Benskin had said that he did not know his piece and therefore he would get part way through it before fainting and falling off the stage. This was hard to believe; indeed it was almost impossible to believe but, in the hope that it would happen, we were tremendously excited.

Late in the proceedings, Benskin came on stage. The Head, who was really quite vain about the status of the school, was almost certainly basking in the reflected glory of having a Classics scholar and a Greek orator on his stage, in his school, in front of a hundred or so impressionable parents.

Benskin began his oration. I recall that he spoke quite steadily. He was not impassioned or overly dramatic but he did move towards the edge of the stage a couple of times. We held our breath – though on reflection I think that he was probably looking for the best landing place.

Finally, he moved towards the edge of the stage, put his hand to his head and toppled, out of our sight, to land on top of the dignitaries sitting in the front row. The stage was high and the fall was dangerous.

His fall was followed by frantic activity as he was carried out of the hall and presumably up to the matron's nursing ward. Eventually the Head was able to make a brief but comforting statement about his recovery. An audible sigh of relief went up from the assembled parents.

If only they had known.

Mr Benskin, sir, if ever you read this, thank you. You were wonderful.

The Company Medical

My second job after leaving school was as a clerk in the motor-claims department of the General Accident Fire and Life Assurance Corporation in Bradford. There were four of us in the department, plus a manager who had his own office at the end of the room.

We were all men other than Miss White, a maiden lady of middle years. Miss White dressed like a Dresden doll in pinks and whites, with many stiff flouncy petticoats under a very full skirt. She attended the manager for dictation and, as she left or returned to her desk, there would be a great sound of rustling fabrics as she manoeuvred her garments into position. Sadly for me, Miss White believed that the department belonged to her and for the first few months she criticised me mercilessly with a sharp tongue.

A week or two after arriving, I was told that an appointment had been made for me with the company doctor. I was to undergo a medical at 10.30 the following morning. This was required of all new staff. I left the office at about 10am and walked through the city to the doctor's surgery, which was opposite the Registry Office in Manor Row.

At this time, I was a callow youth of about nineteen years of age, which in today's terms is probably the equivalent of a twelve year old. I had been in surgeries before but none like this. The room was large, carpeted and wood panelled, and the doctor was silver haired and elegant. He sat behind an impressive desk and was attended by a glamorous nurse.

Despite my youth – and increasing my nervousness – he addressed me as Mr McBurney. I cannot remember the details of the examination, but I do remember at its conclusion being handed a large clear flask and being asked to provide a sample. I was so embarrassed that this proved to be impossible. 'Never mind, this often happens. Come back tomorrow at the same time.'

When I announced at 10am the following morning that I had to go back to the surgery, Miss White's prurient interest was aroused considerably. Understandably, I felt unable to explain the reason for a second visit and for several uncomfortable minutes I suffered some intrusive questioning.

I arrived at the surgery and was met by the nurse, who showed me into a large panelled toilet and then stood outside making unhelpful suggestions such as, 'Have you tried whistling?' Once more, I failed to perform. My embarrassment must have been painfully evident.

'Why not come back first thing in the morning before you go to work?' the nurse suggested.

That evening I consulted Nana, our font of all wisdom on matters medical. She prescribed lemon and barley water. The following morning, I drank enormous volumes of lemon and barley water before catching the bus into town. Opposite the surgery was a café and, on the spur of the moment and despite urgent discomfort, I drank a pint of orange juice.

Somehow, I crossed the road, climbed the steps and burst into the surgery. 'Quickly! Quickly!'

To give him credit, the doctor read the situation immediately and handed me a flask as I reached the desk. No time for embarrassment; I urinated like an elephant. The flask was large but halfway through it was obvious that I would need a second one. Between us we managed a very successful changeover and I carried on for some time before, I think, nearly filling the second flask.

At the end, evidently impressed, the doctor said, 'Well, Mr McBurney, I think that this is a local record.'

General Accident Fire and Life Assurance Corporation - The Office

F ellow clerks Gordon and Phil tried to teach me how to smoke a pipe. Gordon used to take his pipe out to talk, and a curved line of spittle would hang between his pipe stem and his lips. Maybe he talked in short sentences and put his pipe back in between them because I can never remember the spittle falling. He was a good-natured man, kind and funny. He tried to persuade me that in order to develop a calloused thumb, with which to tamp down burning tobacco in the pipe bowl, one should practise on the hot plate of an electric oven, gradually increasing the heat and contact time until the pain became bearable. He also suggested that it was important to begin one's pipe-smoking career with a really cheap briar so that the melted varnish ran down the outside of the bowl. I cannot remember what his logic was behind this, but I do remember the detail.

When I'd been there for some time Miss White, having finally accepted me, even to the extent of once telling me that she liked exciting underwear, a new manager arrived.

He had come from the West Country, a big, awkward, slow-speaking but lovely man. He had big hands and feet, a rough tweed suit and enormous clunky shoes, just like Mr Crabtree from the *Mr Crabtree Goes Fishing* books. He was gentle in his manner, courteous, and presumably completely out of his comfort zone. We were told that he had an incurable condition and that this promotion would ensure a better pension for him and his family. I think that his family had remained in the West Country for the time being. He had to learn to drive and he told me that he was buying a little car.

He was the sort of person that one meets rarely in life but, having met him, one feels enriched. He seemed to handle the workload very easily and, although Miss White hated change and therefore hated him, he never showed any impatience with her. We would hear his soft accent as he walked around his office, taking his pipe in and out of his mouth and thanking her for something, or asking her to take a letter as she threw herself in or out of his office.

Of course, she only hated him until she loved him, which happened after a week or two with surprising suddenness. Her conversion was absolute and then she protected him with every breath.

At some point there was a 'leaving do'. It might even have been my leaving do – I can't remember. It took place in a pub in Ivegate, where generally the clientele was no better than it needed to be. I think it was probably a Friday lunchtime. Late in the proceedings, after I had drunk several pints of beer, a kind lady with one eye said to me, 'You come with me, luv, and I'll see you're all right.'

It seems that Gordon heard this and had the presence of mind to catch me at the door and drag me back into the pub, where he gave me a lecture about the effect that this would have on my mother – or maybe, because he was the 'responsible adult', it was about the effect my mother would have on him.

Pipe Smoking

When I was young, lots of men smoked a pipe. It was generally thought to be a rather manly thing to do. Naturally, being a thing that was almost entirely exclusive to men, it involved a certain mystique. Men judged, and were judged, not only by the type of pipe but by the type of tobacco that they smoked. Pipes could be made of Meerschaum, which looked like a creamy stone and was usually carved into animal heads or the like. Men who smoked Meerschaum pipes were thought of as slightly showy unless, of course, they came from 'abroad', which in our minds was indicated by the wearing of leather trousers.

The majority of men smoked briar pipes, which came in a wide range of shapes and sizes. The best of them were greatly prized and expensive. They improved with age.

There were many pipe tobaccos to choose from. St Bruno was a favourite. I was told that many smokers started with St Bruno then tried several more esoteric brands before finally returning to St Bruno. The indications were that *real* men smoked St. Bruno.

My own favourite was called Rich Dark Honeydew. As an impressionable young man, it was certainly the name rather than the flavour which captivated me, though I remember that the smell from the tin was delicious.

One of the men in the office smoked a tobacco called Erinmore. The joke was that the ladies loved it. It was thought to smell better than it tasted and therefore he was teased quite a lot. He put up with this in a good-natured way and would say things such as, 'Well, it works. You should try it.'

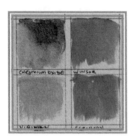

CHROMIUM OXIDE | WINSOR

VIRIDIAN | PTHALO

Diary

7th February–
14th February 2018

February 2018

Wednesday 7th

I have neglected my diary for some days. I have been writing mostly autobiographical recollections and the days, cold and wet, have melded into each other and into weeks with the feeling that nothing very much has happened. How wrong that is.

The political news is confusing and horrific. The Conservatives are in disarray and May is clinging on to power without being able to exercise it. Rees-Mogg, seemingly leading a power group behind the throne, is quoted as citing Professor Minford of Cardiff, who says that a fall in manufacturing output of thirty-plus percent should not frighten us. He goes on to say that our future lies with high-tech service industries, such as design, marketing and IT. If I understand Rees-Mogg correctly, he is agreeing with forecasters who say that conventional manufacturing industry will virtually disappear if we have a hard Brexit. If this should happen, where will the funding for research and development come from? At the moment, much of it comes from conventional industry.

The vision of millions of men and women being out of work because they don't qualify for high-tech jobs is horrifying. This may come soon enough without the intervention of the hard-line Brexiteers. Surely the greater good comes from protecting those, here and now, for whom this 'wonderful new world' holds no promise.

This morning, on the top path in Hawksworth Wood, I found the severed foot and part of the leg of a deer. I brought it home with me. Somehow it seemed wrong just to leave it lying there. Thinking about this poor animal has exercised me greatly. Initially I assumed that the leg had been bitten through by a dog. When I looked carefully, it might have been cut by a knife.

I have only ever seen a couple of deer in the wood, despite having walked there most mornings for several years.

I phoned the council rangers' office just to let them know. I don't know what I expected them to do but somehow I felt that something should be done. They agreed that it was upsetting and told me that people do find parts of animals from time to time. I spoke to somebody else who walks dogs; he told me that he had found bolts from crossbows in the wood.

This beautiful elongated foot sits on my desk as I write. It has softened since I brought it in from the cold. The colour and texture of the fur and the narrowness of the leg is exactly like that of my border terrier.

I think of the years that this wild creature lived in the wood, relying completely on its own instincts. I feel as if it is my responsibility to honour it, to record its death in some way other than this writing. I think, for me, this would mean drawing, painting or photographing. Maybe that would be macabre. No easy answer.

Wednesday 14th

I was peeling potatoes at the kitchen sink when Ruby banged into my legs. I looked down and saw that she was having a fit. She had dragged herself across the floor to me, her legs were splayed out, and she was twitching and jerking. I picked her up and carried her to her bed. I lay down on the floor next to her and stroked her and talked calmly, trying to reassure her until her fit had finished. Her eyes were open all the time. It probably lasted five minutes or a little longer. It doesn't sound very long but it feels long whilst it's happening and it's horrible.

Afterwards we both sat on the sofa and went to sleep for an hour in the gathering darkness. Sue came into the room and we decided to put Ruby into the bedroom where it was dark and quiet.

Later that evening, at about ten o'clock, she went to bed normally but at about two o'clock in the morning she came into the bedroom and climbed on top of me before falling asleep. Though she weighs under nine kilograms, she felt surprisingly heavy and I kept moving towards the edge of the bed whilst pushing her towards the centre. As a result, I had a bad night perched mostly on the very edge of the mattress. Ruby seemed very comfortable in the middle of the duvet!

Ruby hadn't had a fit for a year and I had started to think that she'd grown out of them. It is such a disappointment that this isn't the case. I'm sure that all pet owners will understand our sense of helplessness that this poor little animal should be so distressed, presumably with no understanding of what is happening to her. It's very touching that she struggles to reach me when a fit begins, and frustrating that there is so little that we can do to help her.

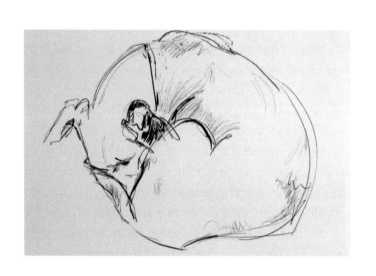

Memories
National Service

National Service Commission

Iwas commissioned as best cadet in my intake of officer cadets, Royal Army Service Corps. I did get the impression that I wasn't necessarily the natural first choice amongst my peers. Somebody told me that the drill sergeant had lobbied hard on my behalf, so it may be that I commanded the Passing-Out Parade and received the Cane of Honour simply because I lifted my knees higher than anyone else.

We rehearsed the passing-out parade on a daily basis for a couple of weeks. It was during this time that the drill sergeant probably realised that he had made an error of judgement in recommending me.

When giving commands to a group of marching man who might be a hundred yards away, an allowance has to be made for the time it takes for the voice to travel and for the men to hear it and react appropriately. The correct timing of the command is vital. My timing was dreadful. When I gave the order 'Parade Halt' at the top of my voice, some men halted and some men kept going. Of course, the men who kept going didn't go very far, as they collided with the men who had stopped.

The drill sergeants were beside themselves with frustration. The quality of the parade would reflect directly on them and their professionalism. Despite all their advice, things got worse as I lost confidence and eventually lost my voice.

I was advised that raw eggs swallowed whole were good for the voice. I swallowed lots of them over a period of several days. I don't think that they helped my voice but I became severely constipated.

On the big day, the parade went much as expected: as the men marched onto the square and as I shouted a strangled 'Parade Halt' with my usual bad timing, those who heard it tried to stop and the rest kept going. Some men took several seconds to regain their composure. The result was untidy.

After that, things improved. The only additional error that I can remember is that I forgot to salute the inspecting officer, a Major General. Fortunately few people noticed.

Eventually we all marched off to St George's Church for the Commissioning Service, at the conclusion of which I was a Second Lieutenant, National Service, in the Royal Army Service Corps.

Headquarters Subaltern

My first posting was as Headquarters Subaltern to 1 Training Battalion, Royal Army Service Corps in Aldershot.

My first company commander was Major Tony Grimshaw, an affable and tolerant man who was kinder to me than I deserved. He was an exceptional horseman and I believe that he had been an Olympic reserve rider. He told me with some pride that he still held the horse and rider high-jump record, I think though I'm not sure, for Scandinavia.

He told me a marvellous story about the then Duke of Westminster. It seems that at some time previously, Major Grimshaw had been ADC to the Duke. He spoke about the Duke's estate in the West of Scotland, and it seems that the Duke had business interests in America. He told me that the Duke had modified a bomber aircraft to carry additional fuel tanks instead of bombs so that he could cross the Atlantic in one hop. Though it sounds unlikely, I'm sure that he said that the plane was modified with floats so that it could take off from the loch on the estate.

He went on to tell me that the Duke's estate owned Grosvenor Square, where the American embassy was situated. The Americans were very keen to buy the freehold of the property and presumably they put pressure on the factors. The Duke's response was to say that in the past his family had owned land in America which had been taken from them; if the Americans would consider returning this land, he would look favourably upon their request. Major Grimshaw told me that the Americans got pretty excited and requested coordinates. These were provided – and shown to embrace the greater part of Florida. Nothing more was heard.

My own day-to-day responsibilities were largely administrative. Though I had no legal experience, and though I had received no training, I was the defending officer in a number of Courts Martial. These were mostly to do with relatively minor offences and usually involved the preparation of pleas in mitigation.

I once defended a soldier on quite a serious assault charge. He had been in a fight with another soldier and was accused of hitting him with a block of wood. Of course, he told me that he was not guilty. The prosecuting officer called a doctor. In his evidence, the doctor stated that the victim would have been unconscious after the blow to his head. As no one but the accused had seen the victim at the time of the incident, I seized upon this in cross-examination. Having challenged the doctor about his unsupported opinion in my best Perry Mason manner, I received a short but heated lecture that put me firmly in my place. As I looked at the Judge Advocate and the Officers of the Court and saw not one shred of empathy, I realised that it was back to the plea in mitigation.

I saw a number of National Service soldiers who were desperate to get home. Invariably they were having marital problems and, if possible, it was my job to help them. This usually involved writing a letter to the local SSAFA Sister in their area and asking for a recommendation. In nearly every case it was suggested that the soldier should be released from his obligation to the army and sent home. This usually happened; I think that the authorities were very good about it.

The Wedding Invitation

In the Officers' Mess after lunch, most of us would go through from the dining room to a large ante-room full of old leather armchairs, where coffee was served and newspapers read.

I had only been in the Mess for a month or two. Harold Riley, the Salford artist, had probably been there for a year. Whatever the detail, I was a new boy and Harold, a larger-than-life character, was an old hand.

One day I heard Harold say, 'I know someone who hasn't read Part One Orders.'

This attracted my attention because I rarely looked at the noticeboard. I waited.

'That someone is Second Lieutenant McBurney.'

Trying to avoid attention, I waited for a moment before approaching Harold and asking what he was talking about.

'It's about the invitation.'

'What invitation?'

'To Major Lloyd's wedding.'

I knew nothing about this and said so. Harold's reply was to the effect that, had I read Part One Orders regularly,

I would have known about this two weeks ago. He went on to say that the junior officers who lived in Mess (that is everyone other than me) had clubbed together and bought a wedding present. Naïve and gullible, I asked if I could belatedly make a contribution. Regrettably, so regrettably, Harold told me that unfortunately the gift had already been engraved with the contributing officers' names.

There followed a muted conversation, in which Harold pointed out to me what bad form I had shown in ignoring this generous invitation to all of us who lived in Mess. His recommendation was that I should explain myself and apologise to Major Lloyd, who was sitting at the far side of the room hidden behind his newspaper.

At the time, officers of field rank were treated with great respect by Junior Subalterns and therefore I approached this task with considerable trepidation.

I started to cross the room, but Harold called me back. 'Be careful. It's his second marriage and he's very embarrassed about it.'

I set off again.

'Bob,' Harold said.

I stopped.

'You'll have to speak up, he's quite deaf.'

I stood in front of Major Lloyd and began to make discreet coughing noises. I continued for a moment or two without success and then increased the volume. Major Lloyd lowered his newspaper and looked at me. 'What is it McBurney?' he said irritably.

'Sir, I want to apologise about the invitation.'

'What invitation? What on earth are you talking about?'

At that moment I realised that Harold, though correct about the embarrassment had grossly underestimated its degree. I had no option but to continue. I plunged on. 'The invitation to your wedding, sir,' I said loudly.

Major Lloyd looked horribly confused. The sweat was running down my face. Moments passed. I felt as if the earth was opening up. We were locked in an impossible situation.

Eventually, Major Lloyd spoke. 'McBurney, I've been married for twenty-three years.'

I remember thinking, 'My God, he's in complete denial.'

After a few more moments of excruciating embarrassment Major Lloyd realised what was happening. 'Bloody Harold Riley,' he shouted.

Most people in the room were crying with laughter.

I can laugh now – but it's taken fifty years.

Though Harold had a wicked sense of humour, he became a good friend. He was kind and helpful to me after I left the army. It's a very long time since we met but I will always think of him with affection.

Mons Officer Cadet School

I soon discovered that my five pounds a week salary as a National Serviceman fell short of my ten pounds a week Mess bill. I decided to apply for a short service commission (the salary being ten pounds a week) and I went to Mons Officer Cadet School.

The Adjutant at Mons was an extraordinarily tall man. I remember seeing him on his parade horse. His feet hung down so far below its belly that the total effect brought a smile to one's face.

One day, on a foot parade, I was standing to attention in the front rank awaiting inspection. Regimental Sergeant Major Lynch of – I think – the Irish Guards, an impressive man almost as wide as he was tall, moved along the line until he stood in front of me. He was tall, but not quite as tall as me. He looked me in the eye and rocked up and down on his toes, sizing me up. To his immediate right, within touching distance, was the Adjutant.

RSM Lynch addressed me. 'How tall are you, sir?'

'Six foot two, sir.'

'Are you sure, sir?'

'Yes, sir.'

'Good,' he said, 'because the Adjutant is six foot five and nobody is taller than the Adjutant.'

On another occasion we rehearsed the Queen's Birthday Parade. It seemed that thousands of us were on parade. It began in the early morning, one inspection after another, starting with the junior NCOs and working up through the ranks, until finally RSM Lynch ascended the dais in the centre of the square.

I think that he might have used a microphone because his voice reached every corner of the parade ground, though he spoke at normal level. His accent was flat and hard. His words were chilling. 'Good morning, gentlemen. Today we are going to work until the steam rises from our bodies.' Immediately following this announcement, he looked over into the distance to his right and said, 'That man moved.'

I can't imagine that anyone knew who he meant, but drill sergeants shouted orders and an entire rank of men was arrested and marched off the square to the Guard Room at high speed.

I suspect that they had an easier morning than the rest of us. There was a popular saying in the army: 'Bullshit baffles brains'. There was another saying: 'Sometimes you've got to laugh'.

Mark 1 Land Rover

My first vehicle was a Mark 1 Land Rover, which I bought for £120 whilst I was serving in Germany.

At the time I was quite ignorant of mechanical things and, despite the Land Rover losing oil, I set off on a very long drive to a forward ammunition depot where I had been sent on detachment. I was in Wuppertal and I think that my destination must have been near the northern part of the border with East Germany.

It was a bitterly cold winter and I had to stop at nearly every garage to buy oil. As I left the urban areas, the landscape became more desolate. I didn't see another vehicle; it was as if the whole area was in suspension. My memory is of featureless countryside, flat and frozen.

Deep into my journey, I stopped at an isolated garage for fuel and oil. I was served by a woman who, bundled in coats and scarves and hat, mistakenly put diesel in my petrol tank. I realised what had happened and she beckoned me to follow her inside the adjoining building.

Inside was an astonishing sight. A huge, drunken man in trousers and singlet was operating a forge and beating metal. Hanging over the fire was a skinned hare. It was like a mediaeval inferno. The heat and colour and his rage at being interrupted were in such contrast to the frozen quietness of the outside world that it was impossible not to be shocked.

He stamped outside and, virtually naked to the waist, lay down in the snow and took the plug out of my fuel tank, drained it, replaced the plug and then went back inside without a word.

The woman filled my tank with petrol. I hoped that she wouldn't charge me but of course she did.

By this time, I was almost penniless and so I was very relieved when I arrived at the village which was close to my destination. I saw a group of young men and asked them for directions. They offered to show me the way and, before I could think of a reasonable excuse, three of them climbed into my vehicle. They knew that I would have cigarettes and soon enough I realised from their behaviour that they might well rob me. I was in uniform and I had a pistol, which I made sure that they saw. Though I had been stupid to let them into the vehicle, the pistol helped; eventually, with a gift of a packet or two of cigarettes, they left me at the edge of a wood, having told me that they had seen soldiers there.

It was dark. I drove up a track into the wood until, to my surprise, I saw a cottage. Surrounded by trees in a small glade, it was single-storey with a pretty porch and snow on the roof. The curtains were open and the lights were on. It was the perfect fairy-tale cottage, and in the dark wood it looked magical. I parked the Land Rover on the track and walked through the trees to ask for help.

I stood in the porch and knocked on the door. Through the glass I saw an old woman. To my horror, as I knocked she started to run around the room in panic. Her long hair was flying about and she was obviously in great distress.

I didn't know what to do. The drive, the cold, the forge and the threats had taken their toll. I was tired, anxious and frightened. If someone at that moment had told me that the woman in the house was a witch, I would have believed them. Actually, for a moment or two I think I did believe that I was in a dream. Unfortunately it was all very real and, despite her terror and my anxiety, I had to stay and sort it out.

Eventually she came to the door and I saw that she was blind, which might be why she didn't have curtains. Despite the language difficulty, somehow I reassured her and she said something about military in the wood.

I was very shaken as I left her and pleased eventually to find some Dutch soldiers who were on manoeuvres and able to direct me to my destination.

I stayed on detachment for some months. I was there when my daughter Stevie was born, so this happened in the winter of 1964–65.

The Alvis

I have always loved old motor cars and I have owned quite a number of them. None of them were expensive but all of them were wonderful in their different ways.

In the early sixties I came back to Bisley from Germany with a military shooting party. During my stay, I bought a 1938 4.38 litre Alvis Speed 25 for £150. I couldn't really afford it but, as is often the case in situations like this, I fell in love with it and simply had to have it. It was a beautiful car, a large elegant saloon with two spare wheels, one mounted in each front wing, and enormous P100 headlights.

Shortly after collecting it, and whilst driving along the South Coast Road towards the ferry, the exhaust pipe came away from the manifold on the engine. The noise was unbelievable. Fortunately, it was in the days before police radio communications were as universal as they are now. As it was, policemen heard me coming from a distance and several times one of them ran into the road to stop me as I passed through various towns and villages. My technique was to slow right down and shout that I was looking for a garage. In most cases, the policeman indicated that there was a garage round the next corner, or in half a mile or so, and I shouted my thanks and thundered on.

Eventually I reached the ferry but was not allowed to load my car without correct documentation, which included an MOT certificate. These had only been introduced recently and I pleaded, to no avail, to be allowed on without one. I then had to find a garage that would do the MOT – which included a road test.

I waited for the inspector to return. When he did, he was very shaken. He told me that on the emergency braking test the car, rather than stopping, had merely slowed down gradually so that by the time it had come to a halt the bonnet was virtually under the tailgate of a lorry. These were fairly cavalier days for motorists and naturally I thought that he should have made allowances and been more careful. He was quite upset and told me that the emergency halt had scarcely registered on the Tapley meter. He also told me that one of the side lightbulbs was inoperative. I thought that this was being 'a bit picky'.

As I was on the point of leaving the country, I appealed to his better nature and suggested that he might be prepared to overlook these minor faults, all of which would be addressed as soon as I got the car to Germany.

Unfortunately he refused my certificate and I had no alternative but to take the car to Aldershot and leave it in a garage behind the Officers' Mess.

The details of this journey have mostly been forgotten, except that I know that I had a puncture somewhere along the Hog's Back between Guildford and Aldershot. I think that the Alvis had been standing unused for some time before I bought it and the inner tubes might have perished. The puncture on the Hog's Back followed several previous ones, which had been repaired in garages en route. The Alvis had a hydraulic jacking system; to operate it, one side of the bonnet was opened and a small tommy bar slotted into a socket on the bulkhead. This was 'pumped' by hand, causing four tubular feet, one at each corner, to descend and lift the car off the road. I did all of this successfully and changed the wheel. Unfortunately, when I released the tommy bar and opened the valve, the car stayed where it was; in the air with all four wheels off the road.

By this time it was mid evening and I was very tired. I was miles from anywhere with an enormous motorcar that showed no inclination to descend to ground level. I decided that there was nothing I could do until the morning so I stretched out on the back seat and went to sleep.

During the night, the car must have descended slowly because, when I awoke, the tyres were touching the road. I had a spade in the boot and was able to lever the feet up a bit more, then eventually drive to Aldershot.

I left the car in a garage behind the Officers' Mess. It was so long that the bonnet protruded from the garage by several feet and unfortunately created an obstacle for other drivers trying to get to their garages.

I returned to Germany. Within days, my company commander started to receive terse messages from senior officers in Aldershot who wanted me to move my car. Fortunately a junior officer friend of mine was able to move the Alvis to a local farmer's barn. I was very grateful for this but sadly it meant that I had to pay rent, which I could ill afford.

Months passed and, predictably, I fell behind with the rent. Then I became too embarrassed to contact the farmer and finally, to my shame, I did nothing until my return to England some years later. When finally I contacted the farmer, he told me that he had needed the space. Not knowing how to contact me, he had placed advertisements in the local papers until, having satisfied the legal requirements, he was in a position to sell the car. This he had done.

I've never blamed the farmer for what he did, nor do I do so now. I behaved badly and he behaved correctly. However, I have often wondered who bought the car and what happened to it. I hope that it found a good home. It would be wonderful if it were still alive and well! Its registration was DWK822.

PERYLENE VIOLET | PAYNES GREY
CARBAZOLE VIOLET | NEUTRAL TINT

Diary

4th March–
21st March 2018

March 2018

Sunday 4th

Walked in the woods with Peter and Ruby. Snow melting slowly. We found four beautiful little snowmen beside the path in Hawksworth Wood.

I have been watching YouTube videos of an artist I admire called Richard Pikesley. In one of them he talks about Rembrandt and a visit to the Rijksmuseum in Amsterdam. He mentions a big crowd in front of *The Night Watch* and says that he 'looked and walked away'. Immediately afterwards he entered another gallery and came face to face with Rembrandt's *The Jewish Bride*, a painting that previously he had only seen in reproduction. At this point he describes himself as being so moved that he burst into tears. He explains his reaction as being the result of the scale and presence of the painting, its physicality and the tenderness of the subject.

I am sure that what he says is absolutely true but I suspect that there is an additional element to the experience, which I think is probably his unguardedness at that moment. It could be that he was preoccupied with being crowded out from *The Night Watch*, something that many of us have experienced. Whatever the reason, he was surprised, unprepared. Had he seen *The Jewish Bride* from a distance and approached it knowingly, he might eventually have been moved to tears – but to burst into tears is different.

I'm interested in his experience because something similar happened to me.

Years ago, I was walking around the Tate Gallery. As I was about to leave, almost as a final act, I turned and looked behind me. On the side wall of the doorway I had just walked through I saw a floral painting by Bomberg. I was quite unprepared for the power of the image, which hit me like a punch. For an extraordinary few moments I knew everything about that painting: its construction, its intricacies, its perfection. I knew beyond doubt that it was one of the most significant works in the Tate. I thought about all the Old Masters in the main galleries, and I despaired that this extraordinary work should be partially hidden and not displayed centre stage.

I needed to talk to somebody about it. The only person available was a guard by the exit. Feeling rather foolish, I tried to share my enthusiasm with him. He was courteous, and I think amused, though I didn't get the impression that he was going to rush off and organise changes in the display.

On another occasion I went to an exhibition of watercolours in a local hotel. I was nervous because I knew the artist. Although I wasn't enthusiastic about the work, I feared that I might be expected to buy a painting. As I walked down some steps into the exhibition room, I was relieved to see a panel of small coloured drawings, one of which delighted me. It was a loose representation of some sheep standing near a tree in a green field. I remember thinking how much can be achieved by such a simple technique, and how sophisticated was the overall result.

After I had looked round, the artist approached me and asked if there was anything that I liked. I enthused about the little sheep picture. I'm not sure who was the most surprised – me, the artist, his partner, or their six-year-old daughter whose painting it was.

I bought the painting for a very modest amount. They did try to give it to me, but I hoped that getting a small amount of money for her picture would make a nice memory for the little girl.

I mention these incidents because I think that when we are unguarded, off-balance, we are particularly vulnerable (sometimes in a rather wonderful way) to experiencing emotions in an extraordinarily powerful way. In this case I'm thinking about visual influences, though I know that in similar circumstances verbal influences are equally powerful.

At its simplest, it is like catching an unexpected glimpse of oneself in a shop window. For most of us this isn't a good experience. When we *choose* to look at our reflection, despite the two reflections being the same, our reaction will normally be very different. How important it is (sometimes) to have all our defence mechanisms in place!

I have never seen the Bomberg picture again. I have seen reproductions of it but, try as I might, I have never recaptured the intensity of that moment in the Tate Gallery.

I still have the little sheep picture. In part, knowledge has spoiled it for me.

I cannot speak for Richard Pikesley. I can only guess that the enormity of his experience with *The Jewish Bride* will be something that he continues to treasure.

It is thanks to him that I have chosen to talk about my own experiences. On both occasions, because of the surprise in one case and the anxiety in the other, it was as if my 'emotional centre' was exposed. Information, unsullied by experience or expectation, penetrated deeply. I think that I saw and experienced emotions with the intensity of a young child.

Now, from time to time, I find myself standing in front of pictures saying to myself, 'I'm open, I'm ready,' waiting in hope for that rush of understanding.

Monday 5th

Most mornings I walk through the woods with my dog, Ruby. If I am alone I talk to myself or rather I write in my head. Occasionally the sentences flow, complete and elegant, and I hope against hope that I will be able to remember them verbatim when I return home. Sometimes

I dictate into my phone using Speech Texter, but this can be a mixed blessing as Speech Texter often introduces creative efforts of its own to harmonise (or otherwise) with my ideas.

This morning my thoughts began with a recollection of the time last year when I was rather smugly feeling international in a vicarious sort of way. My walking pole was climbing Mount Olympus in the hands of Dean, my son-in-law, and my dinner jacket was adorning a friend, Jed, at a wedding in America.

On returning home, I decided to write about this and referred to my telephone notes. As feared, Speech Texter had embellished them. I quote:

'Dinner jacket adorning whimsy deprecating humans sound fully formed lyric which text has made on my Bass Face.'

From Dean, I have learned that if you are planning to climb Mount Olympus there are three routes to choose from: easy, intermediate and difficult. The easy route sounds as if buses might run on it and the difficult route is full-scale mountaineering, so sensibly Dean and his friends chose the intermediate route.

At the risk of sounding facile, I was relating this choice of route to my own autobiographical writings, which are designed to live alongside this diary.

From Sue I learned that adults who experience a difficult childhood can have very poor recall of their early years; in my own case I have found this to be true. Additionally, I have found that one memory jogs the next into being; for the first time in my adult life I am thinking about memories that have 'popped up' from nowhere and surprised me.

Of course the amusing and whimsical memories share space with the painful ones; the stupid mistakes (in my case usually alcohol fuelled), the acts of cowardice, moral or physical, and the many acts of omission.

Having acknowledged these failings in myself, I have to decide how to deal with the whole life through autobiography. I have no remit to write about others, particularly those who are alive and close to me, and when I do so it will invariably be with affection. So essentially this has to be about my own experiences. I don't want to be bland, nor am I in the psychiatrist's chair, so I too choose a middle road. From time to time, I think that I am being too flippant and then I remind myself that although humour is often the public cloak of pain, it may be that the occasional belly laugh is not subject to the same rule.

Tuesday 6th

Conversations between me and Sue are often like TV news discussions with foreign correspondents on the far side of the world. The studio asks the question, we hear it, but the correspondent's facial expression remains unchanged for several seconds before the response is given. The effect is very similar to conversations that take place in this house between the partially deaf (me), and the softly spoken (Sue).

This morning Sue announced that she was going shopping for gym trousers. She said that she wanted something 'plain' and not with 'wee bot' on the back.

I recognised the danger immediately. I paused and thought before saying, 'Sorry, could you say that again?'

'Reebok,' was the reply.

This sort of exchange happens daily. Occasionally other people are involved; I remember the look of surprise on a friend's face when Sue was enthusing about the Fens and he mistook 'big skies' for 'pigsties'.

One of my memorable misunderstanding was to do with the railways. When I was a young man, it seemed that every little railway station in the country was the pride and joy of a stationmaster. Everything that could be painted was painted gaily; flower beds were full of colour, and stationmasters all seemed to be as avuncular as Bernard Cribbins in *The Railway Children*.

A decade ago these heady days came flooding back to me when I was on a train out of London visiting a boatyard on the Thames. As we approached a rural station, a message over the loudspeaker advised passengers that on alighting they should 'take care of the blackthorn hedge'.

A wave of nostalgia engulfed me. I was thrilled. How could I have lost faith? I peered out of the window hoping to see the green shoots. Needless to say, just before the train stopped the repeat announcement changed everything. 'Beware of the platform edge' brought the dream to a sad end.

Thursday 8th

A dog is a wonderful calling card. As I walk Ruby, I speak to people who normally I would pass by. This morning, a man clearing snow from his drive. A smile; a conversation; walking on with a good feeling, a lightening of mood.

Later in the walk I met a younger man and his dog. Large and gloomy, he walked towards me. At the last moment his dog stopped and rolled onto her back submissively. I laughed because it's usually Ruby who does this. After a few facial convulsions, the man started to relax and eventually laughed with me. It's difficult to remain in 'hard man pose' when your dog is waving her legs in the air and tumbling about like a break dancer.

Soon we were both laughing and talking about our dogs. Big face, big smile, soft on the inside.

I talked to Sue about this. She knew exactly what I meant because today she listened to a programme with Clare Balding featuring a new owner with a lurcher dog who walked through central London every day and found that she had to talk to nearly everyone she met. It is like that with a dog.

I think of the time before I had Ruby. If I was walking in the dark with few people about, I would cross a road in order to reduce any imagined threat that I might pose to a single woman. I used to hate the idea that just by being there I might frighten someone else. Now, thanks to Ruby and her innate curiosity, it is much more likely that any chance meeting will result in a few seconds' chat and a smile on departure.

On several occasions I have crossed paths with people who are complete strangers to me but who greet Ruby by name. A lady, who I think lives quite close to us, once greeted me in the street and told me that for several years she and her granddaughter have come to our garden gate to say hello to Ruby. It seems that this is an important routine every time her granddaughter visits. I am laughing as I write this because it seems wonderful that Ruby has a social life of which I am unaware.

Robert McBurney

Friday 9th

I've never felt old enough to wear a Trilby hat. I like hats and I have a number of them (when I was in my twenties, quite ridiculously I had a bowler hat). The problem seems to be that I cannot take myself seriously enough to go around imitating grown-ups. My grandfather wore a Trilby and my father wore a Trilby, yet when I wear one I feel very self-conscious.

At seventy-eight years of age, this presents me with a problem. When, I wonder, will adulthood arrive? Will it arrive? I certainly feel more grown up with the passing of the years but, as far as hats are concerned, I know that I'm not there yet.

Until recently I felt that I had all the time in the world to do those things that I wanted to do, which is really a rather sneaky way of saying that I could put off doing things that needed to be done. Now I am beginning to think in terms of years rather than lifetimes.

All this might seem of little concern were it not for the three Trilbies sitting on the shelf. One is a traditional Panama; one is a rather nice vintage hat, and the last one is a new, very rakish felt.

You see, I haven't given up but the bit of Yorkshire that has rubbed off on me says that if adulthood ever comes my way, will I have time to get 'the wear' out of my hats?

Tuesday 13th

Another virus. Spent much of the night propped up on a pile of pillows, coughing as quietly as I could and hoping not to disturb Sue.

Telephoned Louise, who told me that Ken, our brother, died on this day eleven years ago. It's hard for both of us but we share some memories and talk about him for a few minutes.

Later we talk about our various involvements in the visual arts. Louise bemoans the fact that, as a printmaker, it seems pointless to make just one print but having made several she then wonders what to do with them. I joke that she could put them under the hearth rug as our mother used to do. It's not really a joke because we realise that there are millions of older people drawing, painting in watercolours, painting in oils, writing novels, writing scripts, a huge percentage of which will lie undisturbed until somebody, probably not the author, disposes of them.

I feel quite sorry for that person who has to destroy family artworks. Out of respect for their parents, most children would probably decide to keep things even though they might take up valuable space and never be looked at. After all, it feels disloyal to throw away something that one of your parents made and valued.

I discussed this with Sue, who thought that grandchildren would be able to get rid of things. Unfortunately she went on to say that she had always found it quite impossible to get rid of her own grandma's Harlequin tea set.

We wondered if it might eventually be down to great-grandchildren. It occurred to me that by their time these artworks, however feeble, might have acquired historical significance. Additionally, I realised that each generation might add many millions of new artworks to the stockpile.

I can't think of a solution to this problem, nor can I understand how a simple humorous aside with my sister has assumed such proportions in my mind. It could be that I have a mild fever. Hopefully that will help to explain everything.

Tuesday 20th
Sadly, a few days ago Stephen Hawking died. Amongst the many serious obituaries in the media there were some humorous moments. Indeed, he was described by Eddie Redmayne, the actor who portrayed him in film, as 'the funniest man I have ever had the pleasure to meet'.

At one point I saw a clip from a television sketch where Stephen Hawking was shown alongside Isaac Newton and Albert Einstein. He was making an amusingly derogatory remark to Newton which I think was 'not the apple story again!'.

As I walked Ruby this morning, this cameo prompted the following childish thoughts. Firstly, it seems to me that Einstein got so involved in mathematical formulae that he failed to note that time passes more quickly as we get older – unless, of course, one is waiting for a vital hospital appointment in which case, with a sort of vindictive edge, time slows down again.

As to Newton, and the presumably apocryphal story, allow me to be even more silly. Imagine that, whilst sitting in his mother's garden prior to the apple episode, he needed to go to the loo. Let us say that he arrived at the door of the shed (I guess it would be a shed) to find that it was occupied. He waited; one can imagine him being irritated. Once inside, with bad grace, he peed up the wall like a little boy. (All little boys do this. Some more successfully than others.) Let's assume that the arc made by the urine, its deceleration and acceleration, coupled with its change of direction, exercised his mind.

He returned to his seat in the garden and the apple fell on his head.

Now, let us imagine how things could have been different. No delay at the shed door. A swift return to his seat. Finish his latte and off on a walk with the dog. Plop. The apple falls on the grass. Unnoticed.

So, we could have had a new legend called 'Newton's Quandary', in which he goes on to develop his theory based upon the urine arc. Initially he decides not to publish for fear of ridicule, but then a friend comes to his aid by suggesting the apple story. It's not nearly as interesting but it's 'nice'. Relief all round.

As I walk, I think about this nonsense and any possible relevance. Dog walking features large in my life, and I decide that peeing uphill could be an appropriate metaphor for trying to lead a successful life in the creative arts.

Wednesday 21st

Within the family, I am often accused of eating quickly. The explanation usually given on my behalf is that I am the eldest of five siblings, and that my habits were affected by rationing after the Second World War.

At that time we were four children rather than five as Louise, the youngest, was not born until the late fifties. That apart, the rest of the story is probably true because I'm sure that we were hungry for much of the time.

Eggy bread was a staple part of our diet. It was a wartime favourite with lots of families. An egg (usually just one) would be mixed with milk; bread was dipped into the liquid and then fried. I seem to remember that flavouring was spread on the bread to make it more interesting. I'm not sure what this was – it might have been Marmite.

I know that beef dripping played a big part in our diet. I remember the brown bits in the dripping being particularly tasty, though I can't remember whether or not dripping was eaten with eggy bread.

I once heard Maisie boasting about how long she could make one egg last. In later life I joked with her that she would try to feed a family of six for a fortnight on one egg. She didn't share my humour; I think it was rather too close to home.

Visitors always brought food. For many years after the war it was unthinkable to call on someone without a small gift of food. Should a visitor arrive at mealtime, however inconvenient, a place would always be found at the table. If food had already been served, a small amount would be taken from everyone's plate to make up an additional meal. Though I am unaware of it, this may account for the speed with which I attack my plate!

I was probably six or seven years of age when Maisie took me up the road from Kiln Hill to a small row of houses near the shop where we got our weekly groceries. In one of the houses a family (that I didn't know) had received a food parcel from Canada. I remember that everyone was very excited. There were seven or eight adults there. I was the only child.

I cannot remember what the parcel contained but I do remember that one of the last things to be discovered was a fresh peach. The adults (who were probably all salivating) couldn't decide who should eat it. Eventually someone said, 'Let the child have it.' This was accepted as the best solution; undoubtedly it diffused what might have been a difficult situation.

Someone gave the peach to me and the adults crowded around to watch me eat it and, I assume, to enjoy the experience vicariously. I took a bite out of the peach. The hairiness of it shocked me and I'm afraid that I spat it out.

As one, the adults turned on me. Unkind things were said. I particularly remember someone saying, 'The ungrateful little wretch!' I assume that my mother was embarrassed and we left soon afterwards.

When I think about it now, I realise how young the adults were, probably in their mid to late twenties. Fresh fruit was a rarity, and it may be that most of them had never tasted a fresh peach in their life.

My father had a friend whom we called Uncle Joe. Like my father, he was a company representative. He was a single man. Uncle Joe had two lunches a week with some other family friends and two lunches a week with us, for which he paid Maisie ten shillings. Maisie has often said that Joe's ten shillings 'saved her life on more than one occasion'.

Whatever the weather, ice and snow or full summer heat, Joe always wore a hairy three-piece tweed suit with clunky leather brogues. He owned two elderly Wolseley cars, which he used in turn and polished and maintained with great care. He was a modest man, kind but humourless. Though I think we all loved him, we teased him as well.

Despite being no more than seven or eight years of age, my sister Mary had a very dry sense of humour. One day she was ten minutes late for lunch. As she sat down, someone asked where she had been. Without any expression and very matter of factly she said, 'I've just been outside kicking Joe's car.' Then she began to eat her lunch.

We all knew that she was teasing poor Joe and I think that Joe half knew it, though he couldn't be certain. My guess is that he was dying to go outside and check his beloved Wolseley, but the fear of being the butt of family amusement kept him uncomfortably in his seat until the end of the meal.

Memories

Resignation, Civilian Life

Oliver's Zip

My platoon was on a NATO manoeuvre somewhere in North Rhine Westphalia. We had been held in a wooded location for more than a week, waiting for instructions to move. We had been allowed to stand down for a recreational day.

I was sitting by the campfire when, out of the dark, a small group of slightly tipsy and giggling soldiers approached. 'What is going on?' I asked.

'It's Driver Oliver, sir. He's got his foreskin caught in his zip fastener.'

'Will he be able to get it out?'

'He's tried, sir.'

'Take him away, drink a can of beer and try again.'

Soon they were back.

'It's no good, sir.'

It seems that in order to keep warm Driver Oliver had put his combat kit on over his pyjamas. He was wearing so many layers of clothing that, in the cold and the dark and with a couple of beers inside him, he had made a fairly serious error of judgement whilst doing up the large zip fastener of his combat trousers.

Though I chose not to look, I was told that the part of Driver Oliver that was on the wrong side of the zip slider looked like bubble-gum.

We drove for hours to get to a military hospital. The duty doctor, after some head scratching, decided that a spray anaesthetic and a nail file would be the best tools to use in order to open up the zip slider.

The driver and I sat in the reception, wincing throughout the procedure. Though we couldn't see anything we could certainly hear. The procedure went like this: two sprays of anaesthetic; several abrasive strokes of the nail file; heartfelt groan from Driver Oliver, followed by two sprays of anaesthetic, etc, etc.

It took a long time to cut through the zip and, though he was relatively uninjured, Driver Oliver suffered from considerable swelling. We sent him home to England on leave. He was newly married and he contacted his friends in the platoon to say that he was having difficulty in convincing his wife of the true nature of his affliction.

Resignation

When my children were very young, we lived in married quarters in Germany. I bought a 35mm camera, a Voigtlander Bessamatic, and in a relatively short space of time fell head over heels in love with photography. I read every book available and I knew, without any doubt, that I wanted to be professional photographer.

At that time, I was a substantive Captain but a part of me (the part that wasn't already rushing round the world for *Life* magazine) knew that I was not the 'real stuff' that career soldiers are made of.

Almost certainly because of the lack of privilege in my own background, I never felt comfortable with what I perceived to be the social divisiveness that existed between commissioned and non-commissioned soldiers. Though it is easy to criticise the army on lots of levels, it would be stupid of me to criticise the army because of this. In the 1960s it was how things were. The majority of my brother officers were sincere, hard-working and responsible men; it was me who had become the square peg in a round hole.

Initially I had been conscripted. Determined to make my National Service a positive experience, I had earned a commission. There is no doubt that the sudden change in status from clerk to officer seduced me. Initially I was enthusiastic but later I began to drift. One thing led to another: promotions, postings, and the realisation that I wasn't serving the best interests of the army or myself. I drank too much. I was depressed. When I look back on those days, I realise how depressed I must have been. I slept heavily; sometimes, when I was on my own, I would sleep through a weekend and still be late for parade on Monday morning.

Photography seemed to offer me an alternative lifestyle. Against all the best advice from brother officers, friends and family, and with no income and no gratuity, I decided to resign my commission.

This took several months and was difficult for me and inconvenient for the army. One after another, in order of seniority, company, regimental and brigade officers interviewed me and tried to persuade me to change my mind. They put a lot of pressure on me. At one point a senior officer said, 'Do you realise, McBurney, that what you are doing is tantamount to kicking Her Majesty the Queen in the crotch?'

Finally I was interviewed by Brigadier Greene. I will always remember feeling quite sorry for him because at one point, in sheer frustration at my stubbornness, he said, 'Well, you're a bloody awful officer anyway,' followed immediately by, 'No, you're not. I didn't mean that.' By this time, he was probably more right than he realised.

Then followed weeks of waiting in isolation until my release came through. I remember how extraordinary those weeks were. Suddenly I became 'persona non grata'; I was denied access to the most trivial things, as if I had become a threat or a non-person.

If you are not with us you are against us. No middle ground.

Rude Awakenings, Civilian Life

Clutching your camera and saying 'I am a photojournalist' is all very well if you are actually taking pictures that have a market. Fortunately I did have one good client, the Manchester *Guardian*. Brian Redhead was the editor and he became a wonderful supporter, giving me as much freelance work as he could. But even his best efforts were not enough to keep the wolf from the door. Fees were modest and often my mileage returns were greater than those from my photographs.

It was impossible to get other work without a union card. Brian proposed me to the NUJ and I was seconded by an ex-president of the NUJ, but this was still not enough. I was in a Catch-22 situation: if I couldn't prove that I was making an adequate living from journalism, I couldn't get an NUJ card; without a card, I couldn't get the work.

I was in Brian's office when he heard that he had got the *Today* job. He was so excited. In my ignorance, I couldn't understand how anything could be better than being the editor of the Manchester *Guardian*. I lost touch with him after that and later I heard of his early death with great sadness.

For the first few months my wife Jackie, my two children and I relied heavily on the generosity of Jackie's mother. It was obvious that things could not go on as they were and, under some pressure, I went to the local executive employment exchange in Bradford. I hoped to try and find the sort of job that would 'tide me over', as the saying goes.

My credentials were clear enough: I was a fully qualified small arms instructor; I could handle explosives; I was experienced in running military transport.

My interviewer at the executive exchange seemed impressed with these qualifications and made careful notes. He then offered me a job gutting chickens on a production line in Shipley. This was not what I had imagined though, in fairness, he did point out that there weren't many opportunities for weapons handling in Bradford at that time.

I had thought that my transport experience would be useful, but it seemed that there were subtle differences between civilian haulage companies and dragging Corporal missiles around Germany.

The interviewer was considerate. He advised me indirectly against taking the chicken-gutting position. He told me that most people didn't last too long in the job. It seems that a moment's inattention and the hooked blade of the gutting knife enters the ball of the thumb. This is followed by a course of painful injections. Most people do not return to work afterwards.

Shortly after this fruitless experience, my mother-in-law said that she knew someone who could give me some part-time work as a taxi driver in Shipley. This seemed a sensible way of earning some money whilst leaving time to attract some clients and develop my photographic business.

Taxi Driving

In practice, driving taxis on a part-time basis in order to do other things was not the solution to my needs. Other drivers working shifts relied upon me being available at specific times. Occasionally these times clashed with photographic assignments. In truth, the photographic assignments were few and far between and gradually the driving took over.

The owner of the firm had a fleet in Keighley and I spent some time there before being offered the opportunity of taking over a car in Skipton. There was just the one car in Skipton and the driver was no longer available, having been locked up for non-payment of maintenance. Being on my own in Skipton, and therefore being able to take time out without inconveniencing anybody else, seemed like a good idea.

Again, things did not work out as I had hoped.

Moving to Skipton, which I did with my family, isolated me geographically as far as photographic clients were concerned. It was probably at this time that I realised that my situation had become desperate. The only ready source of income that I had was my taxi. I decided that, for the time being at least, I would put all my efforts into building up a taxi company.

I worked night and day; never in my life have I worked so hard. I had a camp bed in the office. I was on duty seven nights and six and a half days per week. Even though I lived less than two miles from the office, I only went home for a few hours on Sunday afternoons.

In truth, I cannot remember how long this lasted. Eventually I had other cars and drivers. Life certainly became easier but I always worked very long hours. I ran the company for several years. We became well established but, however hard we worked, it was always a hand-to-mouth affair. We were undercapitalised and the wear and tear on our cars was a constant drain on our income.

The experience of taxi driving is equivalent to that of a masterclass in human behaviour. One sees the very best and very worst of people, often in the same twenty-four-hour period. On Friday night, young men full of bravado and Timothy Taylor's bitter were being carried to their front doors, only to reappear on Sunday morning wearing their best suits and looking nervous as they headed for the church.

Some of our best clients were Pakistanis, many of whom lived down Station Road in Skipton. At the time, there was some news about differences between East and West Pakistan, though I can't remember the details. I had four Pakistani men in the car and I was heading down Keighley Road. In innocence – and ignorance – I explained to them that I didn't know the difference between the two groups.

They knew me quite well and they all laughed. They told me that they came from West Pakistan.

I asked if there were any East Pakistanis in Skipton. 'Oh yes,' they said. 'We are going to pass some sitting outside the mill as we go down this road.'

'Is there a difference? Would I know it?'

Quite seriously one of them said, 'You would – they are all small and brown and they all look just the same.'

With no disrespect to them, I hope that my Pakistani ex-clients would acknowledge the truth of what follows.

It seemed unthinkable that any one of them could undertake a taxi journey on their own without the support of friends and extended family. I remember arriving at the house of a client to take somebody to the railway station. At first the patriarch came out and sat in the front passenger seat. He was followed by other male members of the family, who took seats in the back in order of status. I was allowed to carry four passengers. As four people were already in the back seat, it took time and effort before I was able to get the extra person out of the car.

Despite the grumbling and the appeals, I was ready to move off. 'Where are we going?'

'To the station but not yet. We're waiting for Grandma.'

Eventually Grandma came out of the house. She was the traveller; she was going back to Pakistan and the men of the family were there as escorts – or for the ride.

Eventually the most junior male was evicted and Grandma took her place. We set off for the railway station. Halfway to our destination someone, presumably the senior male, said, 'How much to Leeds?'

We were busy because it was Easter and it was inconvenient to go to Leeds. I remember putting up a spirited resistance but gradually being worn down by the persistent pleas and persuasion from the rest of the car. Eventually I gave in and we headed to Leeds. Halfway to Leeds, it began again. 'How much to London?'

To cut the story short, I drove to London – not once but three times during that Easter long weekend.

There is no doubt that we drove when we were tired, sometimes when we were exhausted. Fortunately there were no accidents, other than the occasional scrape.

Finally, I handed over the business to John, my foreman driver. I was very relieved to get away. John took over the business on a rental-purchase agreement. He kept up the payments for several months but eventually he had to tell me that he couldn't manage any more. I wasn't surprised. He was a good man and a friend, and I'm sure that he had done everything that he could.

It's easy to remember the fun bits and the humour. It's probably fortunate that one forgets most of the drudgery, the punctures in the middle of the night, the clutches burning out, the clients who took you twenty miles up the Dales at night, only to disappear after going to get the money.

I try to be generous with taxi drivers; usually they are working when I'm playing. I think that to be a driver in the city is certainly more financially rewarding than to be a driver in the countryside. I also think that drivers in the city have to put up with abuse and violence of a kind that we never knew. Recently I travelled from Leeds to Horsforth by taxi and I was surprised at the sturdiness of the plastic cage that isolated and protected the driver. Times have changed.

Phobia

I have a long history of injection phobia. It began in childhood when I spent periods in hospital. As a child I fainted often. I remember being told that I had fits and that sometimes I was unconscious for quite some time.

My clearest memory of hospital is an episode that lasted for several weeks.

Whilst I was there, I had several injections every day, which I remember resisting. For some reason I was in an adult ward; I had a cot in the centre of the ward. The staff apologised for this, acknowledging that I was too old to be in a cot but explaining that it was the safest place for me.

I really have no idea why I was in an adult ward; on reflection, it was ill-advised. I remember my shock at seeing a large older man swinging his legs out of bed and inadvertently exposing himself as his nightshirt opened. His scrotum was a bruised purple colour and getting on for the size of a house brick. Coming from a prudish family, and never having seen adult flesh, this sight made a marked impression upon me. Seventy-five years on I'm afraid that (with a shudder) I can still visualise it.

Whilst I was in hospital, I was tested for allergies. I have a memory of injections in my thighs, labelled with the name of the product written on my skin. Around each injection a small circle of pinpricks with spots of blood. Though my memory has faded over time, this used to be a very strong visual image and I know that my phobic reaction to injections relates to this early experience.

Certainly injections had become a major problem by the time I was called up to do my National Service.

As basic recruits, we were stripped to our underpants and a long line of us shuffled towards medical orderlies who injected us in turn. As a matter of pride, I wanted to survive the experience unscathed.

I think that we were injected several times. Immediately afterwards I was hugely relieved because I was still on my feet and feeling shaken but OK. I was just congratulating myself when I went into shock, after which I remember nothing. It seems that as I fell, jets of sweat splashed those people who were standing near me.

Later I was told that orderlies carried me into an adjoining room and tried to towel me down. I have no recall of re-joining the group but I was told that I was so wet through with sweat that several other men fainted, thinking that the orderlies had used buckets of cold water to revive me.

A year or two later, when I was on manoeuvre in Germany, an accident involving a piece of wire left me with a small cut in my eyeball. The pain was intense and eventually became unbearable. A driver took me to a local town and we were able to wake up a doctor.

I suspect that the doctor was tired and not a little distressed at being woken up, and I think that she was quite rough with me. I lay on a couch and she peered at my eye. Without explanation, she took hold of my eyeball with her fingers. I was so shocked that I fainted.

When I woke up, she was very critical. She said that I had frightened her 'very much' when I fainted. 'I had to inject you in your heart to wake you up.'

'In my heart?' I said, not really believing such a thing possible.

'Yes. Directly in your heart.'

I remember my sense of incredulity just before I fainted again.

Dentistry became a nightmare. I would explain to dentists that I was phobic. Over the years, most of them would tell me that 'it wouldn't hurt'. In turn, I would tell them that it was absolutely nothing to do with pain.

This might sound far-fetched. Far from it. When the shock hit me, I had to get out of the dentist's chair and kneel on the floor. The sensation was that of a tremendous weight forcing me down; I would describe it as feeling like a load of wet sand was being tipped onto me. During these times I never lost consciousness, and whilst it was happening I would be explaining to the dentist that it wouldn't last long and that I would be back in the chair soon. I would be saturated with sweat.

One dentist, who had assured me that I didn't know the difference between a phobic reaction and understandable nervousness, was so upset that he shouted at me never to come into his surgery again. He shouted several times that he thought I was going to die. His assistant was sobbing in the corner. I think that I left without treatment.

Eventually I found a dentist who recognised my problem and gave me an armful of Valium before further injections. I have no recall of the treatment at all and for a long time I believed that I had been unconscious throughout. I've been told that this volume of Valium was almost as dangerous as the shock, but at the time I was very grateful.

When my father had his first heart attack, the doctor who attended him gave him an injection. At the back of my mind I have always had the fear that, even if I survived a heart attack, the shock of the injection would probably kill me.

I told my wife Sue about this. As I remember it her response was, 'If it happens, I'm sure that you will be able to deal with it.' This conversation took place ten years ago. Sue tells me now that there was more to it than I remember, and that she used low-level hypnotic techniques.

It is difficult to over-emphasise the effect that my phobia has had on my life and it is almost unbelievable to me that Sue was able to lift it from me and to cure me completely.

Blood tests and flu jabs, minor injections, no longer trouble me. I cannot pretend that I like the injections at the dentist's but I can cope with them. I am so grateful to Sue – and yet I really don't understand the process in my brain by which it has happened. How was it possible to overcome something that was so powerful and so entrenched? It seems improbable that words alone could effect such a massive change, and yet there is no doubt that this is what happened.

Kenneth Michael

My younger brother Ken was a musician and artist. During his teenage and young adult life I was away, initially at school and then in the army, so I didn't see very much of him during this time.

I know that he left school with very little sense of direction and that a family friend suggested he applied to Bradford College of Art, where he was accepted by the college on condition that he continued to study in order to meet their academic entry requirement.

Whilst at college, Ken developed a very individual style of painting in oils which involved using his finger wrapped in a rag rather than a brush. He painted on hardboard, which was primed with several coats of Dulux white undercoat. He claimed that only this paint gave him a flat finish with enough tooth to accept the oil paint.

He painted thinly, in glazes, building up density with repeated applications of colour. His paintings were virtually monochromatic and the colour he used was an earth colour, called Van Dyke Brown. He had to keep the painting wet whilst he worked, so each painting would usually involve a marathon session of working through the night. If he left the painting unfinished, he had to cover it in damp cloths until he returned to it.

Occasionally he would be persuaded to add hints of another colour, possibly even two other colours to a painting, then he would grumble that the whole thing looked like a rainbow.

Ken loved old buildings. Most of his paintings were of old stone buildings and cobbled streets, places like Haworth and Wycoller and the Calder Valley. I bought a painting from him. It was the first one that he sold and I bought it at his first exhibition. I am looking at it now as I write, a dark, brooding image of a deserted house in Wycoller.

Ken had a good friend in Bradford called Graham Bell and Graham's parents, Dr and Mrs Bell, championed Kenneth's paintings. Friends of theirs became patrons and, at a later date, the Brontë Society of America commissioned a painting from him.

At a later date still, our father represented him for a short time. He placed paintings in galleries throughout the North and the Midlands on a sale-or-return basis. He worked on a commission from sales but I don't think he ever understood the emotional effort that it took Ken to paint. As far as our father was concerned, painting was a simple application of craft; if galleries wanted more colour, that's what you gave them.

Over the years, the act of painting seemed to become more difficult for Ken. When Dulux stopped producing the undercoat which he preferred, he regarded it as a personal affront. Van Dyck Brown was a highly toxic earth pigment made out of decayed organic material and other unknown substances, which made it a potential hazard to health. The manufacturers withdrew it. Ken was incensed; he regarded it as an attempt to prevent him following his trade. He contacted all the main colour men, who tried to assure him that similar pigments were available that made perfectly good substitutes. Ken was not convinced, and rightly so.

Earth pigment paints have individual physical qualities. For example, Van Dyck Brown was transparent, whereas most other dark-brown pigments are opaque. Additionally, when you feel the paint through your fingertip as you apply it you will certainly recognise differences in touch.

Even so, I suspect that Ken was looking for an excuse not to paint.

It was during his time at art college that Ken became involved with a theatre company, which I think was the Red Ladder Theatre Company. Ken was a skilful guitarist and he began writing music for them. He taught himself to read and write music; for some years from then on, he composed and produced scores for a number of instruments. I did not see these but my sister Louise tells me that the scores were beautifully finished and presented.

Ken married a girl called Jacquie. They had a baby, Claire, and they lived in a flat in Bradford. They were desperately short of money and the landlord terrorised them both. I remember visiting them; they were shaking with fright, thinking that it was him knocking on the door. They used to call him Rat-face. I don't know the circumstances but possibly 'Rat-face' deserves some sympathy because I am sure that the rent would have been in arrears!

It was probably inevitable that they would separate. I was with Ken when Jacquie and Claire left. All that I remember is their overwhelming sense of resignation. No tears, just a sad goodbye.

Ken played a professional season as bass guitarist with Paul and Barry Ryan, the sons of the singer Marion Ryan. He also played with the Mike Westbrook Jazz Band at Ronnie Scott's on a couple of occasions. At some point after that he met a German woman, Gabi, and they returned to Germany together where Ken lived for the next sixteen years. During these years he had a small studio, which he described as being underground with a window at pavement level out of which he could peer at people's passing feet. Most of his work seems to have been realistic drawings which were fairly 'tight', seemingly at the request of his clients. He also made household furniture for several friends.

After the initial honeymoon period, the relationship seems to have stalled. Ken would phone occasionally and sound very depressed. I suspect that his mental health deteriorated; certainly, he was drinking a lot. Once when he came to stay with me he brought a half-bottle of malt whiskey, ostensibly as a gift, which he opened on arrival. During the week he stayed with me, he worked his way through my drinks cupboard, taking a small amount from each bottle in turn. By the end of the week every bottle was down to the last half inch.

When he eventually phoned to say that Gabi had asked him to leave, our mother Maisie was desperately upset. I tried to reassure her that Ken would be all right, that we would look after him. She knew Ken as well as anyone, and she was inconsolable.

When Ken arrived in England, he was in despair. Eventually, after we realised that no degree of illness or distress would qualify him quickly for assistance, Maisie bought a small old wooden motorboat in which he could live. It was out of the water at Methley Bridge Boat Club. She did this because my Dutch barge *Longfellow* was moored there and, though I wasn't living on it, she knew that I could keep an eye on him.

Ken's boat had a small solid-fuel stove in the main cabin. There were gaps in the planking and in the deck; it must often have been cold during winter weather, particularly when the stove went out. Ken was a hard man to help. When I learned that water was dripping through the deck and onto his bunk, I gave him a tarpaulin. Though I left it lying folded on his front deck, he never found the energy or motivation to unfold it. Eventually he was treated for frostbite in his feet.

Then followed a period of many years during which Ken's deteriorating situation was so distressing that it is very painful to write about.

When he was living in the boatyard, he spent most of his days in the pub. On several occasions after closing time, he would fall and lie in the road or the yard and remain there until somebody picked him up and carried him to his boat. Despite this, people who lived in their boats were really very kind to him. They often fed him because otherwise he would just have the occasional takeaway. People were fond of him; despite all his problems, he could be good company. With a drink in his hand, and with his dry sense of humour, he was at his best.

My barge was sold and I didn't go to the yard as much. It was a relief not to have to see Ken. As his elder brother I felt both affection and some responsibility for him, but he was still his own man and resented criticism or interference. He never recognised his own drink problem and would become quite angry when challenged on the subject.

Eventually Ken was housed by the Council, initially in a flat in Castleford and later in a bungalow. Though he had money, I don't think he ate very much. His days began with a mug of cider and spirits, from which he sipped all day, topping it up as the level fell. He became an easy touch for others. They would sit and drink with him. One or two of them were genuinely helpful and would shop for him; others would rob him of the few possessions that he had. Homeless people and druggies bullied their way in and used his place as a crash pad.

Ken had a large sheepdog called Ollie, who spent most of his life in the house sitting on a narrow window ledge and barking at passers-by. Ollie became hysterical when Ken had a visitor. I was not used to dogs at that time and I was nervous about Ollie. Ken refused to be separated from him and, as a result, I never felt able to bring Ken to my home where we could have fed him and washed his clothes. Additionally Ollie had fleas and Ken (who had a cruel streak) would say that scratching was a sort of hobby for his dog.

I dreaded visiting Ken. It was always a harrowing experience. After a visit I would stand outside, unable to drive away. Occasionally the grief would be overwhelming.

Towards the end of his life, I visited him and found he had been sleeping in his chair as he was unable to reach his bed. I talked to him about calling an ambulance but he said that one of his friends had done this, and that the ambulancemen had said that he was not ill enough to be taken to hospital. I went out immediately and bought him the most comfortable folding bed that I could find, which I assembled close to his chair.

On my final visit, I found that he had not moved out of his chair for many days. I phoned the ambulance and he was taken to Pontefract Hospital. Time after time as he was leaving, he made me promise to look after Ollie. He told me to take his jacket, which contained all his money and identity documents. The pockets were stuffed with bundles of notes and coins and used lottery tickets.

Ken was in hospital for two weeks. I visited him every day. Ollie went into kennels, was well looked after and eventually found a wonderful home for his old age.

Whilst in hospital Ken was reunited with his daughter.

'Is that really you Claire?'

'Yes, Dad.'

'I haven't seen you for five years. Where have you been?'

'I've been busy.'

'That's all right then.'

Ken had cancer. He was not in pain. Sadly, he died alone during the night. The cleaner found him in the morning.

Mary, Louise and I visited the hospital to see him. Mary and Louise held his hands, one each side of the bed. Mary said, 'Look how beautiful his fingers are.'

Ken was cremated at Rawdon Crematorium. Friends who had known him before his decline came, and we talked about his talent and the sad waste of things.

We had ordered spring flowers for his coffin. After the service, bouquets were hung on a wall in a sheltered walkway outside the building. Mary and Louise and I stood near Ken's bouquet and remarked on how lovely it was. After we had been talking for a moment or two, Mary peered at the name and said, 'This isn't Ken's, it's someone else's.'

We looked at the wall and realised that the bouquets stretched along the wall apparently in decreasing size order. We walked along to the far end where the smallest bouquet was hanging.

'Well, it's very nice.'

'Yes. Anyway, the big ones are a bit showy.'

In the years following Ken's funeral I met several people, usually doctors, who had bought his paintings in the early days following art college.

'You wouldn't be related to Kenneth McBurney, by any chance?' they asked. They were usually mystified as to what had happened to him, how he had disappeared from view, and they were obviously very pleased to own one of his paintings.

It seems appropriate that Ken, as he once was, lives on through his paintings. Young. good-looking, angry enough to qualify as the archetypal creative spirit. All this before the burden of his genetics and experience overpowered him.

Diary

1st April–
30th April 2018

April 2018

Sunday 1st

At five o'clock this morning I woke up unexpectedly. Before going back to sleep I checked my phone to see the result of the heavyweight title fight between Anthony Joshua and Joseph Parker. As expected, Anthony Joshua won by a unanimous points verdict.

I was reminded of a night in May 1955. I was a 'late fifteen' year old and a boarder at Ripon Grammar School. It might have been at a very similar time in the early morning that I and a couple of friends sneaked down from the dormitory to my shared study room to listen to the Don Cockell versus Marciano heavyweight fight on the radio.

Knowing Marciano's reputation, we expected him to beat Don Cockell easily, and indeed it seemed that the fight was very one-sided in Marciano's favour. We feared the worst. Then, as the ringside commentator became quite excited and said things such as 'Cockell is moving forward, he's throwing punches, Marciano is backing away', we too became excited. We huddled around the radio whispering, 'Come on, Don, you can do it,' and similar optimistic comments. Sadly, this was not to last and soon the commentator was saying that Marciano was hitting Cockell at will. We knew that it was nearly all over.

A few days afterwards we saw some of the fight on Pathé news at the cinema in Ripon and realised that Don Cockell, despite tremendous courage, had never really had a chance.

I have just watched the fight on YouTube. The final rounds were so one-sided that they were shocking. Cockell, who was overweight, slow and stubborn, and who seemed virtually indestructible, absorbed terrible punishment. I think it was in the eighth round that the referee stopped the fight on a technical knockout.

The British camp complained about Marciano's head-butting and low blows, though to his great credit Cockell did not join in with this. Despite some legitimate complaints, there is no denying that Marciano was in a different league; his hand speed and his ferocity were extraordinary.

I feel very differently about this fight than I felt when I was fifteen. Now I am horrified by the one-sidedness of it. Many of my friends and family members feel that boxing should be banned, whilst I struggle with the guilty knowledge that championship heavyweight boxing still excites me. Maybe it comes down to contestants being more evenly matched and fights being stopped quickly if they are not.

Thursday 5th

Driving to Harrogate this morning, I passed a war memorial in Pool-in-Wharfedale covered in red poppies. It made me think about bravery and courage. Later in the morning I talked to my granddaughter about this. We discussed the meaning of the words bravery and courage. I thought that bravery might often refer to a specific act, whilst courage could be thought of as a state of mind. I wondered if you have to be truly afraid to be truly brave.

I often think about these things in relation to the First World War. The poets are the only faces that I can picture, but I try to imagine the hundreds of thousands of soldiers who died, many of them blundering forward through the mud in the face of machine-gun fire.

Five years ago, Sue and I voyaged south in motorboat *Juno* through the Netherlands, Belgium and France to the Mediterranean coast. As we travelled down the Meuse valley, the quietness of the countryside, the softness of the contours of the farmland, and an overlying sense of stillness and sadness affected us both.

The night that we moored in Verdun, wedding preparations were taking place. A convoy of cars was driving round the streets sounding horns. People were hanging out of the windows and shouting at each other. We were approached by the bride and her bridesmaids and asked for a donation. In return we received a small gift from the bride. I can't remember what it was; it might have been a flower or a sweet. One of the bridesmaids explained to us that this was traditional in Verdun. It was all cheerful and tremendously noisy.

Earlier that evening I had been walking around the town looking at memorials to the huge number of people who died. The contrast between this experience and the wedding party could not have been greater. In my heart I was thinking, stop the noise, show some respect – and yet I knew that I was being unrealistic. The 1914–18 war was a hundred years ago. Generations have been born and died since then. Another thought also occurred to me: many of the people who died would have done so in the hope that a time would come when the shouts and joys of a wedding party, irritating or not, would return to the streets of Verdun.

Saturday 7th

Went to a party last night. Heard a delightful story. Everyone a little bit drunk, so the laughter was possibly more uproarious than it might otherwise have been. Even so the story was very funny.

It involved two old soldiers, both suffering from constipation and sitting side by side on one of those primitive plank-of-wood, multi-hole lavatory seats. One of the soldiers hears a plop, plop, plop. 'Well, you're lucky,' he says to his companion.

'Nay, not so lucky,' says his friend. 'That were me knife, fork and spoon.'

Tuesday 10th

I have been disturbed by the characterisation of the two lead women in two separate TV programmes, one American, one English, *Homeland* and *Marcella*.

In both cases, week after week, they are shown as causing a degree of emotional trauma to their own children that can only have a long-term damaging effect. Yet at the same time, these women are shown as heroines. Admittedly they are quirky and difficult, but they are heroines nevertheless, doing the best that they can in challenging circumstances. As such, they can be seen as role models – role models who allow their involvement with self and career to hurt their children. Surely this is irresponsible?

Do the writers have any idea about the significance of attachment in children's lives?

My guess is that most parents will be distressed by what they've seen. My fear is that young people might be influenced to think that what they have seen is acceptable behaviour, to mistakenly believe that, when the going gets tough, children can be pushed to one side and they will understand. That children, like adults, will have the capacity to bounce back.

Thursday 12th

On this day, with Donald Trump beating his tweeting finger on the keyboard whilst behind him in the shadows, hawkish generals worldwide secretly limber up their button fingers and dream of military domination, I despair. This awfulness of Syria, this abomination, this international shame.

Helpless, as are we all, I seek solace in avoidance.

Probably because of the posturing of men (it's usually men in these cases), I think about testosterone.

Now, despite it playing a significant part in my life – and it seems in the lives of others – I would be the first to admit that, although I am talking about it, I have no idea what it is or what it looks like. I'm sure that I would be able to distinguish a teaspoonful of testosterone from a similar measure of raspberry jam, but that might be the limit of my appreciation.

Additionally, I have recently become more aware of the dissonance between my self, that is my thinking self, and the physical body that my thinking self inhabits. I have come to realise that I have a lifelong responsibility of care for my body but despite this it is definitely going to let me down. The imbalance of this situation disturbs me.

One might say that the bit that I recognise as 'me' cannot live without the body, but it seems that the body can live or die without 'me'.

At its simplest, I can only watch impotently whilst my fingernails grow; on the other hand, the combination of my body and a liberal splash (or not) of testosterone has had me running around like a blue-arsed fly for half my life and is now trying to turn me into a grumpy old man.

Is all this as it's meant to be? Who thought to install untutored minds into teenage male bodies?

'From hemlock seeds no roses grow.'

Friday 13th

Dear Diary.

I think that this is what you write when you are recording something very secret. Having written the secret, you close the diary and hide it in your room. Sometimes it takes some ingenuity to find a hiding place which you feel is satisfactory, somewhere where your mum won't stumble across the diary and read it. You like to think that your mum won't search your room though, in later life when you are searching your own child's room, you realise that this was probably unrealistic.

All of these things may well be true when you are young, but when you are seventy-eight and writing your diary and you have a fear that you scarcely dare talk about, what do you do? What do I do?

Sue has been to the opticians this morning for an eye test. In doing so, she has made me think about the repeated reminders I have been receiving from the opticians, telling me that the time has come for me to have a test. My last test seems so recent that I find it hard to believe that I'm due for another one. My last test happened because I requested it; I was beginning to see some distortion in the central vision of my left eye. The opticians referred me immediately to the eye department in the hospital. At first it was thought that I had some macular degeneration, but on my third visit the consultant told me that I had macular dystrophy rather than macular degeneration. Degeneration can be treated; dystrophy can not.

From what little I understand of the cause, it seems that macular dystrophy is the result of waste matter within the eyeball clumping together and finding a home on the optic nerve. Since the diagnosis, the distortion in my central version of my left eye has increased. It may well have stabilised now but the result is that I cannot read clearly with that eye.

The consultant told me that there is a possibility, maybe a probability, that the same thing – or macular degeneration – will happen in my right eye. At the moment my right eye seems perfect. Whilst close work is more difficult than it was, for example reading is tiring, my right eye and my brain allow me to see perfectly at mid and far distances.

My mother had macular degeneration in both eyes. For the first few years she had good peripheral vision. She could make sense of the television, though she said that she couldn't distinguish faces. For the first time I am beginning to realise how distressing this must have been for her.

It is only now, when it's happening to me, that I begin to understand.

I am frightened of losing vision in my right eye. I cannot imagine how I might cope if it happens. In the meantime, I eat the correct foods, take supplements, protect my eyes from bright light. All of these things are good, they may help, but they offer no guarantees.

Despite the fact that you, if you are reading this (having sneaked into my room and found my diary hidden under the mattress), are meeting me as a writer, most of my adult life has been concerned with visual imagery. I paint, I draw, I photograph. I use Photoshop. I have a commercial printer in my room. I am surrounded by thousands of books. I build boats and I make furniture for them. In none of these activities do I claim any great reputation, but I do claim that all of them give me tremendous enjoyment. Collectively, they form the backbone of my days. I cannot imagine life without them.

If (I should say when) I go to the opticians there may be further warnings. Therein lies fear.

Monday 16th
Another troubled day in the United Kingdom. Prime Minister May having to justify the rocket attack on Assad's chemical weapons establishments. The threat of a major cyber war from Russia. The Windrush scandal.

Where does it all go? How does it end? Is the public very involved? I think not, but why not?

I remember the Profumo case. Day after day, people were waiting at the news stands for the first edition of the daily paper. It seemed as if the whole nation was enthralled by the proceedings. The case involved ministers, spies, Russians, royalty, sex. Almost certainly it was the prurient sexual details that engaged the nation's interest most intensely, but I think that there was a very real anger that a politician could behave badly and lie to the electorate.

In many ways, I suppose that the public interest in news is much the same today as it was then. A scandal, a story about celebrity, sexual or financial, seems to excite national interest. I understand why this is so, why it has always been so, but in the past I think that it went hand in hand with a genuine concern for matters of national importance. In addition, naïvely or not, we expected politicians to be truthful. We expected evasions but not outright lies.

Politics is important on a personal level because governments act in our names whether we like it or not. Despite the weariness caused by a never-ending succession of blunders, dangers, threats and acts of incompetence, we have to find the energy to hold the system to account. To allow our expectations to diminish, as we seem to have done, is to expose ourselves to the creeping danger of totalitarianism.

Tuesday 17th

Yesterday in Parliament David Lammy spoke about a day of shame in relation to the Windrush scandal. He might easily have said 'a time of shame', because the scandal has been going on for many months. In addressing Parliament, he said that, 'If you lay with dogs you get fleas.' It is difficult to imagine that he was not addressing Amber Rudd, Minister for the Home Office, and Theresa May, the Prime Minister.

Having read the details and case histories of some of the people involved, I think that the actions of the Home Office have been unforgivable. I believe that the Prime Minister and Amber Rudd have a stain on their names and character that should never be forgotten.

A final thought: the policies that led to the Windrush scandal were put in place because of huge public pressure.

Saturday 28th

A couple of weeks ago I wrote about that part of me which I recognise as 'my self' having to look after my body, which inevitably will let me down. Today I read that scientists at Yale University have restored circulation to the brains of decapitated pigs and kept their organs alive for several hours. They are talking about the possibility of human brains being allocated new bodies when the old ones fail.

I was being a little bit tongue in cheek; now I'm not sure what to think. If it is possible one day to replace exhausted bodies with new ones, it may also be possible to replace perfectly good bodies with more attractive ones. I can see a time when the streets of our cities are full of Brad Pitts, Daniel Craigs and Dwayne Johnsons.

What about women, you ask. If this is not a trick question, it is at least a tricky one. I think that I will take advice, after which I will probably say nothing.

Monday 30th
So, Amber Rudd has resigned from the Home Office. People who worked with her say that she was a good boss. It is true that she was under pressure to continue with policies established by the Prime Minister, but it seems that she did so with enthusiasm. I am reminded of Donovan's song 'The Universal Soldier' in which he says words to the effect that the 'universal soldier really is to blame'.

I think that it is remarkable that the reason given for her resignation was that she inadvertently misled Parliament. I think that many of us would have thought it more honourable for her to have resigned because of the damage and pain that she caused to so many innocent people.

Memories
Family and Adventure

Kenneth's Ashes

We collected Kenneth's ashes from the crematorium. They were to be divided between five of us: Ken's daughter Claire; sister Mary in Cornwall; our mother Maisie; Louise, and me. Additionally, Claire had the idea of scattering some of the ashes in a pub, where, in younger life, Ken had spent many hours at the bar. Louise and I discussed this and we could see that there would be problems. The pub had a rough wooden floor and Louise thought that we might be able to do it by putting ashes down our trouser legs and shaking them out secretly whilst leaning at the bar. We had seen this being done in an escape film but, though it seemed a bold idea, neither of us really wanted Kenneth's ashes in such close proximity to our ankles.

Eventually we decided that we would give the idea additional thought.

The responsibility for dividing the ashes fell to Louise. She took the whole operation very seriously. She wanted to make an exact division as she felt that, in fairness, we should all have an equal 'share of Ken'. She decided that the best way to achieve this was to use her kitchen scales.

Louise was making minor adjustments between the five piles, the scales and the urn when her thirteen-year-old daughter came into the house with a new friend. When asked by her daughter what she was doing, Louise replied, quite matter of factly, that she was dividing up Kenneth's ashes. Her daughter's new friend turned and ran from the house, never to return.

My share of Ken's ashes is in a beautiful earthenware pot that he made at art school. It sits next to his brush holder in the corner of my studio.

Walking in County Cork

As a boy, I was brought up reading a relatively small collection of books. The ones which had the most effect were stories of King Arthur and the Knights of the Round Table and Irish fairy tales which, as one would expect, were all about the warriors, witches and ogres of Irish legend. Memorable stories such as *The Boyhood of Fionn, The Carl of the Drab Coat* and *The Enchanted Cave of Cesh Corran.*

As a young man I read American authors – Mailer, Hemingway, Baldwin, Lowell, etc, and American photographers, particularly Edward Weston, became my abiding inspiration.

I also felt a powerful affinity with Ireland, having been told that my paternal great-grandfather came from there to the Halifax area where his many children went from door to door with trays, selling the sort of knick-knacks that tinkers might have made. It never occurred to me that, being a Protestant, he almost certainly came from the North and so, when I heard of a place in County

Cork called Ballydehob in Roaring Water Bay, which was described to me as an artists' heaven, I had to go.

I left my home in Headingley and caught a coach from Leeds to Liverpool to take the night ferry to Dublin. This was the sort of 'back to roots' journey that we men in our late forties sometimes feel the need to take. I say that in the hope of exciting sympathy for the sorry early part of the tale that follows.

I arrived at the ferry with the clothes in which I stood, a voluminous long white Mac, a small pack with three pairs of underpants, some socks and a bottle of whiskey. Cash in my pocket and no documents at all.

'Passport,' said the bored-looking security officer.

'I'm sorry, I haven't brought it. I didn't think it was necessary as we are all in the Common Market.'

His expression changed. 'What is your name?'

'Robert McBurney.'

'Well, Robert,' he said rather patronisingly, 'you are correct. But have you heard of the Troubles?' Then followed a question-and-answer session in which I think he assumed that I was intellectually challenged. He used simple words in short sentences with lots of emphasis. In truth, he was probably tired and fed up; however, I felt irritated and rather foolish. Finally, he asked me what I did for a living. I told him that I was the chairman of a small group of companies involved in photography and design. Under the circumstances it probably sounded unlikely.

I wish I'd had the courage to ask him if he'd seen John Wayne in the film *The Quiet Man*. You know, the film where John Wayne comes to Ireland wearing a long Mac and that singular big flat cap, and sweeps Maureen O'Hara off her feet. He might better have understood the romanticism of my mindset.

The security people made some calls and established that I was who I said I was. They let me go. Perhaps I'm not being as charitable as I could be; perhaps they too secretly wished that they could walk around Ireland wearing a long white coat and hoping that they might look a little bit like John Wayne.

I believe that they followed me because someone, whom I assumed to be a security person, rather clumsily engaged me in conversation on the coach to Dublin. I think that they were still suspicious.

From Dublin I caught a bus to Cork. In Cork I changed my money in the bank and the teller, handing me my cash, said, 'I think you'll find that's approximately correct.' Which, coming from a banker, I found unnerving.

Friends had told me that greeting anyone you meet in the Irish countryside is really important; not to do so is considered ill-mannered. The greeting takes the form of an abbreviated version of 'how are you' plus a lift of the hand. I took a bus to Ballydehob. After finding a room above a pub, I prepared for my long walk. The first morning I passed a farm where several men were erecting steel frames for some large barns alongside the road. As I passed and greeted them, each man in turn put down his tools, stood up and waved back. I felt like an automaton; it was like a scene from a Chaplin film.

After that I saw very few people. It was early in the year and the couple of people that I saw in their gardens went inside and closed the door quite quickly when they heard my English accent.

I walked for several days, spending my last night in Bantry where I stayed in a hotel in the town centre. I asked if I could have a bath and I was shown the most antiquated bathroom with a huge cast-iron bath surrounded by steaming and gurgling pipes and taps on stilts. Prior to the bath, the landlord gave me a short lecture on its operation before leaving me alone to struggle with the Victorian technology.

One of my abiding memories, and a highlight of the walk, was standing on a headland overlooking the Atlantic one beautiful evening, the grass cropped and green and a sheer drop to the ocean. To my left, spectacular tongues of rock; ahead great rolling waves, powerful and beautiful in the evening light tumbling towards me, finally finding land after a fetch of thousands of miles. Far away, but as close as I could get to the land of my dreams: America. I was quite alone. I felt privileged, even blessed. It was a significant moment.

Then disappointingly, to my right in the distance, there appeared a figure with a sheepdog. I hoped he would go on his way but he approached me and we talked. After a few minutes, he asked me where I was from. I said, 'Leeds.'

At the time, Assistant Chief Constable George Oldfield of Leeds was in charge of the hunt for the Yorkshire Ripper and had recently put out a press release saying that the Ripper had size eight feet. The Shepherd looked at my feet, which are size eleven.

'You'll not be the Ripper,' he said. 'But you'll know him.'

My walk was early in the year and therefore out of season. Finding places to stay was difficult; more often than not, it meant going to a B&B and being redirected to someone who might or might not be open.

I stayed in one house where every room had identical nests of tables. I asked the man, who was retired, what his trade had been. He told me that he had been a cabinet maker. I asked him what he used to make and unsurprisingly he said, 'Nests of tables.' In addition to furniture, every room had an elaborate wall hanging about the evils of drink. His wife was out and I offered him a whiskey, relying on the hope that his contribution to the decor might have stopped with the nests of tables. Not so; a resolute refusal as he rushed out of the room. Having stopped drinking many years later, I now recognise my lack of sensitivity at the time.

Northern Rock

Years ago, Sue and I were afloat in the Netherlands on our first boat *Orca* when Sue's mother telephoned to say that there was a run on the Northern Rock Bank, where all our money was invested.

In a fit of creative fervour, fuelled by helplessness and anxiety, I wrote dozens of limericks. It does seem improbable that limericks were my response to such a serious situation. Anyway, here is one.

A gentleman banker from Leith,
Used a file to sharpen his teeth.
'It's to broaden my smile,
An urbane crocodile,
With a heart of your gold underneath.'

The Gaiety

Tassy's was an upmarket hairdressing salon in Upper Briggate, Leeds. It occupied large premises and operated over several floors. Tassy, who was Greek, was the principal around which the business focused. His brother ran the office. Both of them were very kind to me. For a time, they allowed me to use their top floor rent free as my studio. In return, it was understood that I would always be on hand to photograph styles or models for display.

One evening I was invited to a stylists' night out in the Gaiety pub in Leeds. I had never been to the Gaiety before and my then wife Faye warned me of its colourful reputation, which included topless bar staff.

I remember that we sat at a long table in a large room and that I was at the end which was furthest from the stage. On the stage a female artiste was performing a routine in which her breasts contra-rotated in time to music. She had tassels on each nipple, which added to the decorative effect. I thought that this was a rather wonderful achievement. I was looking down at my beer and, as someone without breasts, I was twitching my shoulders and trying to imagine how one could initiate the movement. After a moment or two I heard her call for a volunteer. I looked up and she was pointing at me. At first I thought that I had been chosen on merit but later I learned that everyone on our table had pointed back at me.

I stood up. It was the last thing I would have chosen to do, but I made my way to the stage to the sound of cheering and laughter. My main thought was that I should make the best of the situation for everyone's sake, so I took off my jacket, twirled it around my head and threw it into the audience. This was much enjoyed and raised expectations to a new level.

The artiste said to me, 'We are going to blow fire.' This was a surprise. What she should have said was, 'You are going to blow fire.' She gave me mouthfuls of fuel and said, 'When you blow, blow like hell.' She held the flame and I blew. Jets of flame shot into the audience. I was really enjoying myself; eventually she had to persuade me to leave the stage.

Later she found me and thanked me. 'You were great, love. It's meant to be surgical spirit but it was three-star.'

On the way out, a bouncer told me that they could use me again any time that I was free. I felt the rather self-satisfied glow of the performer, though what my breath smelled like with a mix of beer and petrol I can only imagine.

Voyage to Whitby

I learned my marine theory at an evening class in Wakefield and my practical boat handling in a narrow boat on the Leeds-Liverpool Canal. With these qualifications, which were legal but shall we say short on the salty side, I set out into the North Sea on our forty-foot steel motor boat *Orca*.

This summer holiday voyage to Whitby, for which we had allowed two weeks, began at Castleford. Sue and I arrived on the Friday evening, ready to leave on the Saturday morning. On arrival, we learned that the lock gates half a mile up the river had been damaged in a collision. They were inoperative and would be so until after an inspection by a surveyor, which would take place on Monday. We camped on the boat and lost two days.

After an overnight stay at Goole we were just about to enter Ocean Lock, which leads into the tidal river Ouse, when we received a phone call to tell us that our house had been burgled. We lost another day.

Hull was uneventful; we lost one day to bad weather.

The weather really closed in at Grimsby and we stayed there for a week. Some places, even Grimsby, can be boring after a few days of forced inactivity and we really wanted to move. We set off on the first day which had a reasonable weather forecast: out through the lock and into the Humber Estuary.

I won't go into all the hazards and buoys which marked our passage from the estuary into the open sea, other than to say that in the estuary, with its sandbanks and channels, one expects lumpy seas and messy wave patterns. Because of the cross-currents we were thrown about quite a lot. Sue was anxious but I was confident that, once clear of the estuary, the sea would be more comfortable.

I was wrong: the day was sunny, the winds were quite light, force three or four, but the seas were big.

By this time, we were several hours out of Grimsby and had to make a decision as to whether we should turn back or go on. The forecast was quite good so, bearing in mind the length of time it would take us to return, I decided to go on.

We stood off the land and headed north along the hostile Yorkshire coast.

Sue became seasick. She lay on the floor, where she remained throughout the day. Without self-steering, I couldn't leave the wheel. *Orca*'s prow would go down the face of a wave, plunge into the sea and throw water back over the wheelhouse as she climbed up the next wave. I had to throttle back to reduce the violence of the motion. As a result, when the tide was at its peak against us, we were making very little headway and progress was slow.

Sue was unable to help. Nevertheless, the sun shone and though *Orca* was probably in her element, I was not. I tried to stay positive by making jokes to myself. I remember thinking what a comfort it is to have a qualified person in charge in conditions like this, and 'I am that person!'

Throughout the early part of the voyage we received several radio messages asking all skippers to keep an eye open for a trawler that was in distress. After hearing this message several times I acknowledged it and explained that I was unable to leave the wheel to check on the coordinates of the trawler – was I anywhere near? The answer was an amused but courteous negative; the trawler was very far north in the fishing grounds. Even so, and despite the sunny day, this grim message added to the general sense of anxiety. (We were very relieved, several days later, to learn that the trawler had been found and that the alarm had been a false one.)

The hours went by and I was very tired. The only distraction was the guillemots. Groups of them, black and white, bobbing about on the sea, would see *Orca* bearing down on them and try to escape. At first, they would run along the surface of the water, flapping their little wings and looking as if they were trying to take off. At the last moment, they would abort the take off and dive away to the side. They seemed so jolly and amusing. I was grateful to them.

In the early evening, after a very long day, we were off Scarborough where we decided to stop. I radioed the harbourmaster and was instructed to go into the commercial harbour. From the sea, silhouetted against the evening sun, Scarborough looked desolate and uninhabited. As we neared the harbour entrance it was astonishing to see hundreds of people, colourful and happy and unaware of our anxiety.

The harbour entrance is quite narrow. As we entered, someone leaned over, smacked the top of the wheelhouse with the flat of his hand and shouted, 'Go over there and tie up next to the trawler.'

Orca is difficult to manoeuvre at slow speeds because large bilge keels were added to her hull some time after her build and these have affected her handling. Because of this, I was very pleased to make a gentle landing on the side of the trawler. I tied up and we took stock. We were both exhausted.

There was another knock on the roof.

'Could you move across the harbour onto that wall?'

'No,' I said. 'I'm too tired to move.'

'Okay,' said the voice. 'It's just that this boat is leaving at four-thirty in the morning.'

Sue was feeling awful and this was more than she could bear. 'Why is this boat such a pig to steer? Why doesn't anybody here know what they're doing?'

There was more.

Believing as I do that boats, even if they are not sentient beings, have personalities and have to be loved, I rushed to *Orca*'s defence. I stroked and patted her instrument panel. '*Orca*, you are a beautiful boat. You got us here safely. I think you're fantastic.'

I was near the limits of my endurance and I was probably a bit hysterical because I didn't stop there. I went on for some time in much the same vein, saying how splendid the harbour was, how nice the people were, how pleased we were to be here.

I was interrupted by a shout from the other side of the harbour. 'Skipper of *Orca*! Skipper of *Orca*!' I leaned out of the wheelhouse door.

'We are delighted, sir, that you love your boat and that you like us so much. Please would you check your radio transmitter.'

I had put the handset down so that it rested on the tumbler switch. I was on Channel 16. Most skippers would have a listening watch on that channel, though I can't imagine that many people outside the Northern Hemisphere would have heard me.

Flash Powder

When I returned to England in the 1960s with the intention of becoming a photographer, it was still possible to buy photographic flash powder. It came in substantial little tins. Thinking about them now, I visualise a grey and orange label and appropriate words of caution, if not warning.

Those were the days when photography shops had things on dusty shelves in dark corners and fortunately I found such a shop, which just happened to have some flash powder. I bought two tins; they might well have been the last two tins in England.

I had read that flash powder gives a beautiful soft light, highly actinic and virtually shadowless. At the time, I imagined that I might be able to use it commercially. Looking back I can't imagine how, but I must have read something that led me down that path. It could be that I lived in hope because in comparison flashbulbs seemed so expensive.

I do remember having read that 'banquet photographers' used flash powder. I also read that they packed up everything ready for a quick exit prior to taking the photograph. This was because a few moments after the flash, a cloud of fine soot would descend upon the table settings – by which time the photographer was hopefully getting into his car, or at least running round the corner of the street. Interesting though this was, I must have realised that 'banquet photographers,' particularly in Bradford, might well have had their day.

I was never too sure how photographers in the past lit the flash powder. Like all of us, I had seen footage of Victorian portrait photographers holding a tray above their heads prior to the enormous flash and bang. I wondered if they'd used a cigarette but this seemed dangerous, almost suicidal.

Fortunately, I found a reference for a flash-powder tray, which incorporated battery ignition, and I had one made out of galvanised metal. It was 300–400mm long and it looked like a shoebox with one side missing. Set into the base were two small upstanding terminals with a fine wire running between them. A tripod screw thread was fitted to the bottom of the tray so that the whole apparatus could stand to one side, a safe distance from the photographer.

In operation, flash powder was spread on the base of the tray, making sure that there was enough to cover the fine wire. At the moment of exposure, a battery connection was made, the wire glowed and ignited the flash powder – or, often enough, it didn't.

There was a fine balance between success and failure. Just enough flash powder in contact with the hot wire gave success; too much powder and ignition was stifled, probably through lack of oxygen.

Even when everything worked nothing happened quickly. It took seconds for the wire to get hot enough to glow and ignite the powder. It was heart-in-the-mouth stuff, dramatic and inconsistent. A failure to ignite was always a cause for concern. One approached the tray expecting the whole thing to go off suddenly, taking one's eyebrows with it.

Despite flash powder being economical, it was an alarming process and certainly something that one would never use in the presence of a client. I enjoyed experimenting with it, and though I never used it on a job, I got through the first tin. I put the second tin away on my own 'dusty shelf in a dark corner' and forgot about it.

Years later, when I was living in Rochester Terrace in Headingley, I read an article which said that flash powder could become unstable if stored for too long. So, on a calm, bright midsummer day, I took my tin of flash powder into the back garden and heaped the powder into a cone shape on a flat stone in the centre of the lawn. I lit the fuse.

I anticipated the ball of intense light but I guessed that it wouldn't attract much attention because of the bright sunshine. I anticipated the sound but I thought that anyone hearing it might think it was a firework. What I did not anticipate was the dark mushroom cloud that rose vertically and steadily into the air, the stalk perpendicular and the mushroom annulus rolling gently. The whole thing looked like a perfect, sinister miniature of the early footage that we saw from Bikini Atoll.

I stood in the kitchen doorway hoping (I almost said praying) that it would disperse.

I may never know whether or not anybody else saw it. Nobody said anything to me. Thankfully Headingley was always a cool place.

Diary
2nd May–30th May 2018

May 2018

Wednesday 2nd

I really shouldn't go on about Donald Trump but the latest revelations by his personal doctor, which state that Donald Trump dictated his own medical appraisal that the doctor then wrote down, beggar belief.

Of course, we knew. Not many doctors would use the phrase 'astonishingly excellent'.

It is possible, assuming that he allows us to live, that Donald Trump, already a legend, will become a 'national treasure' in America. No one else in living memory has provided such a wealth of material for comedians, journalists and news junkies across the world. He may not be a 'cuddly' national treasure, more a Barabbas, but 'our' Barabbas.

I know that it's a serious business really, that I shouldn't laugh, but what else can one do?

Thursday 3rd

Ruby and I were on a quiet road heading for Hawksworth Wood. Walking towards us was an elegant young man wearing headphones. Using both arms, and with a look of intense concentration on his face, he was playing what could only have been a complex drum solo.

At the last moment he looked up and saw me. I smiled with pleasure. Unable to acknowledge me, he looked away. I wanted to talk to him but I knew that it would only add to his embarrassment, so we passed each other without a word.

The whole experience made me think about our concern with appearances. In his situation I would have felt just as embarrassed, and yet what he was doing was wholesome and entertaining.

When I see elderly Chinese people on TV doing their singular exercises in a public park, I am always envious about their apparent lack of self-consciousness.

Monday 7th
Something has prompted me to think about general anaesthesia and surgical procedures!

Being a secret sort of a soul, I have always worried about the possibility or probability of my being indiscreet when waking from anaesthetic. This was brought home to me many years ago when I was trying to help my then-wife Faye to dress after a minor procedure. We were in the corner of a recovery room and we were behind screens. Faye had only recently come round from the anaesthetic and she sounded as if she was very drunk. As we fumbled with her underwear she said in a loud and slurred voice, 'You wouldn't have this trouble if you were trying to get it off.'

Other than a small group of nurses at a desk by the exit door, we were the only people in the room. I could hear laughter. I could imagine what they were saying and thinking: 'That's right, you tell him, love. Useless men, they're all the same. It's all they ever think about.'

Actually, it was funny. I did try to look dignified as we left. The nurses were still laughing. Later on, when I told Faye what had happened, she refused to believe a word of it.

Tuesday 8th

Rather surprisingly (because of its age), I had to take my car in for a manufacturer's recall to a garage in Pool-in-Wharfedale near Leeds. As it was only going to take twenty minutes, I went for a walk. On the opposite side of the road to the garage, tucked into the wall, was an old cast-iron road sign. Incongruously it was probably a hundred yards from the nearest crossroads. Possibly the junction has been moved at some point because the road sign serves no purpose where it is.

On one side of the sign it says Leeds 8 miles, on the other side Otley 2½ miles. What I found particularly interesting and amusing was the top of the sign, which states that the distance to London is 194¼ miles. I have played with the idea that either the maker of this sign had a well-developed sense of humour, or that he was a man of very rigid mindset. Whatever the reason, I am amazed that, before satellite navigation, someone was confident enough to calculate such a distance to within 440 yards (approximately 400m).

Just to be sure, I dialled in the postcode of the garage and 'London' on an Internet route site. I was given three distances according to one's choice of route. They were 205.29 miles, 217.98 miles and 204.81 miles.

Older people often say that things were better in the past; whether one accepts this or not, it seems that travel to London was easier. Obviously, the roads were quieter and London had not moved quite so far away.

Thursday 10th
A late spring. Each day a gift. After the heat of the bank holiday, now a cooler wind. The bluebells are dying back, otherwise everything green is burgeoning and glistening in the sunlight.

In the house we are growing hollyhocks from seeds. Eighteen of them have sprouted. We are clucking over them as if they were babies.

In Iran they are burning the American flag and pictures of Donald Trump.

Blunder and plunder and nuclear thunder, A gun in his hand and hate in his heart...

What a difficult situation for European countries. If we continue to act rationally in supporting the nuclear deal with Iran we are threatened with sanctions by America. What an unthinkable situation.

Monday 14th

One would say that this is a lovely spring day, as indeed it is. Warmth, sunshine, a soft wind and birdsong everywhere.

Yet, as I walk through the wood, mainly because of the volume of noise, I become aware of forces at work all around me. Forces no longer in balance. The sun blindingly bright as it strikes through the trees; the birds noisy, frantic with anxiety. Though I cannot see them, I know that thousands of litres of water are rushing up tree trunks. Movement everywhere, change, enormous tensions, grass that will break through concrete; the life force!

As I walk, I'm trying to think of a more interesting title for this book. Initially, I thought that *Nearly 79* was quite exciting until someone told me that in their opinion it was boring. (How quickly one can lose confidence.)

I added *Laughter and Loss* and then lost confidence in that, I think mainly because *Loss and Laughter* has better cadence – and yet I don't want to emphasise the loss part of it.

Now I'm searching for alternatives.

Accidents of Mirth... too posey!

Testosterone and Raspberry Jam... catchy but not representative of the content.

Two Left Foots... I like it but maybe for something else.

So it goes on until I'm confused and I have to stop without a result.

Maybe back to square one.

Tuesday 22nd

Not cold but windy this morning. Soft sunshine in the wood, the bluebells no longer vivid but reduced to a blue-grey memory of brighter times. The rest of the wood is verdant and bursting with life, so I suppose it must be the bluebells that make me feel melancholy.

Sue and I have been talking about ageing and death. Her mum is in a residential home and is suffering from

Parkinson's and near blindness. Her distress prompts us to talk about our hopes for our own futures, and our wish for an easy death.

Of course, there is no suggestion that we are looking for a way out now or any time soon. Neither of us is quite ready to abandon the hope of immortality. We are just having five minutes of being 'grown up' and 'realistic'. We say things such as 'Wouldn't it be nice not to wake up one morning?' or 'Wouldn't it be nice to die peacefully whilst reading a book?'. After we have frightened ourselves with these relatively painless scenarios, we let the words hang in the air for a few moments before changing the subject and moving on.

It occurs to me that millions and millions of older people are probably having very similar conversations.

Death is such a troubling concept. The more one thinks about it, the more troubling it becomes. How extraordinary life is, and equally how extraordinary that it should be curtailed.

Somewhere I have read, or learned, that people do not like behaving or being made to behave in ways that they cannot justify; nor do they like to live with open-ended questions.

A simple and rather prosaic example of this would be the introduction of seat belts in cars. When seat belts were first proposed, there was an outcry against them. Newspapers carried articles where motorists and some organisations said that they would be dangerous; for example, in the case of accident or fire, it might not be possible to get drivers out of the car quickly. The opposition to their introduction was considerable. Despite this, the government went ahead and the use of seat belts became law. Drivers who had sworn never to wear them had to do so. Very soon those same drivers were saying what a good thing seat belts were. Now it would be unusual to find anyone in their right mind who was opposed to their use in domestic cars.

What, one might ask, has this to do with death?

Well, probably not much other than the similarity of us having to do something (in this case to die) that mostly we don't want to do and the reasons for which we don't understand. To further complicate the issue, although we accept the death of other sentient animals as a simple matter of fact, we have imbued our own deaths with incalculable mystery. As a result of this quandary we have, over centuries, embraced a variety of religions, all of which fortuitously are designed to make us feel better about the whole thing.

This is not to say that many of us embrace death, though it seems that some believers in some religions do.

When it comes to my own death, my position as an agnostic doesn't offer much comfort. In this respect part of me envies devout Christians. They have a surety of place and purpose, one might say both here and there. Maybe it's the ultimate seat belt.

Tuesday 29th

In London. Staying at the Premier Inn Hub, Covent Garden. Room 408. Tiny but very modern and immaculate. I'm surprised by how friendly the staff are, such a change from the indifference I remember from Londoners years ago.

Spent the morning in the National Portrait Gallery. I am very 'taken' by the wild-eyed self-portrait of a young Mervyn Peake. Whenever we discussed literature, my great-aunt Vivy would invariably tell us that she danced with Peake on Sark. I would like to think that, young though she was, it could scarcely have been a romantic interlude. Vivy and her partner, Edith, had met at university, and though they could never be seen to be living together their love was of the most enduring kind. It is said that they met every day of their lives.

Vivy was head teacher at a girls' school in Bradford and, though I only really knew her in her retirement after

Edith had died, I remember her as a wonderfully stylish person – reflecting another age – sitting in her book-lined apartment, sipping sherry and smoking cigarettes through a long holder.

We saw the play *Red,* about Mark Rothko. Everything about it was stunning. I don't think we will ever forget it.

Wednesday 30th

We are in London. Ruby is in Harrogate with my daughter Stevie and her family.

Stevie has just been away with a couple of girlfriends for a short holiday In Portugal. She tells me that she is suffering from sunburn having mistakenly used conditioner instead of sun cream.

Though it is funny when all your liquids and ointments have to be repackaged to satisfy airline security, it's an easy mistake to make. Unfortunately for Stevie, in addition to sunburn she had problems with security on the return flight. Having thought that toothpaste would not be included in the list of regulated items, she had a full baggage search.

The search began with the usual questions: 'Have you packed your bag yourself, are you carrying anything for anyone else?'

Having answered with a confident yes and a no, she watched as her case was emptied on the counter. Quite unexpectedly she saw a pair of men's underpants. It seems that she picked them up with both hands and, holding them high above her head so that her girlfriends could see them, she shouted, 'Whose are these?'

When Stevie told me this story, I wondered if I would be able to repeat it. Fortunately, it seems that the pants belonged to her husband and had been left in the case since a previous holiday.

Back in London, Sue and I have been to see the musical *Tina*. It was an amazing spectacle. The singing was magnificent.

The demographic of the audience was interesting. Though it was international, almost everyone looked to be of a 'certain age'. As a result, during the interval, the queue for the gentleman's loo was long and long-suffering, the faces in the queue alternating between good-humoured resignation and quiet desperation. There may have been another room downstairs, but upstairs there were only three stalls in the loo and progress was slow!

That aside, it was a memorable evening.

As we walked back to the hotel, a homeless man asked me if I had any change. It reminded me of a time when I was a little boy playing in the street outside my nana's house in Carlisle. I was accosted by a tramp, a large rough man. The street was empty, though why he chose me, a small boy unlikely to have money, is a mystery. I am sure that he was trying to frighten me. He asked me if I had the price of a loaf.

At first, I didn't understand what he had said. I was nervous, and his accent and the phrase he used were unfamiliar to me. I cannot remember what I said but I caused him to repeat the question. When he did so, and when I understood what he was asking, I really didn't know what to say. I was a polite boy and I probably felt an obligation to him having, as it were, engaged him in conversation. I do remember that, despite not having any money, my immediate concern was not knowing the price of a loaf.

Undoubtedly an early indication of the 'whiff' of autism that has affected so much of my life.

PERYLEEN GREEN | COBALT

INDANTHRONE | FR. ULTRA

Memories

A Sadness and
More Adventures

Dad's Final Illness

When my father became ill for the final time his initial complaint was a pain in his shoulder. This gradually became worse until he became bedridden and was diagnosed with lung cancer.

As a family, we were very shocked. We put pressure on one or two people we knew to try and get Dad into hospital for treatment. On reflection this was a mistake, though obviously well meant. Had we been given the sort of honest advice that one would expect to receive now, we would have known that he needed palliative care. That would have been so much kinder. As it was, he was taken to Cookridge Hospital and treated with a view to recovery. Recovery was never an option and he died after a painful illness.

It is so easy to be wise after the event, but we did think that we were doing the best thing for him.

Cookridge was not an easy option. I talked to a nurse who told me that patients were expected to fight to get better. I know that Dad had a fall; he was on his way back from the toilet to his bed when he asked for assistance.

He told me that this was refused, and he was told that he had to do it on his own. He fell and broke his pelvis.

When we visited him, he often looked unwashed and unshaven. It may be that my sister Louise shaved him. I could not have done so. He was a man you did not touch.

On the evening he died I was in Manchester on the forecourt of a prestige car garage, photographing an advertisement with an art director and male and female models in DJ and furs. Louise phoned me with a thoughtful message. She knew that I was busy, but when I had finished she thought that I should go to the hospital.

We returned to Leeds and I went to Cookridge Hospital. Louise and Maisie were there. Dad had died in the late afternoon.

I asked to see him. The staff tried to discourage me but I insisted.

They kept me waiting for a short time. Dad was in a small room on a bed. Someone had put his teeth in, but not very accurately as they had distorted his face. It was hard to recognise him.

After all the pain that had passed between us, I thought that the moment should have a special significance. I don't know what I expected. I walked around the bed, trying to breathe evenly, trying to control my emotions. I wanted to talk to him but I couldn't speak. I left knowing that I had failed us both.

My father predeceased his mother. She was in a residential home, high on the moors overlooking Halifax. Maisie and I went to visit her.

After we had talked for a moment or two Maisie, as gently as she could, said to Grandma, 'I have to tell you something very sad. Kenneth has died.'

Grandma looked at Maisie without affection. 'Yes, I heard,' she said. 'Did you kill him?'

And death do stir the pot.

Learning to Ride a Bike

When I was fifty, I decided that I would learn to ride a bicycle. This new mission presented me with the opportunity for a massive amount of research, all of which I took very seriously. After choosing frame, gearing, saddle and bars etc, I ordered a bicycle which was assembled into a lightweight touring machine by an artisan bike shop in Leeds.

I bought a bicycle rack for the car and I bought a tracksuit. I cannot remember whether or not Lycra was the fabric of choice for cyclists thirty years ago, but certainly bright, tight kit was worn by the serious sportsman.

This presented me with a dilemma. I am rather (very) thin, and not seen at my best in shorts or tights. From time to time I imagined myself in the proper gear but then I remembered an occasion many years earlier.

A new wife had fondly said to me, 'I'm going to call you Budgie.' I was flattered because for some reason I associated the name with Adam Faith, who was a significant popstar. Seeking further gratification, I said, 'That's nice. Why have you chosen that name?'

I was astonished when she said, 'It's your legs.' Prompted by the flash of pain which crossed my face, she began to roll around on the floor with tears running down her face, laughing uncontrollably.

Though it's bad form to laugh so much at your own jokes I let it pass, despite being wounded.

So, a floppy tracksuit it was.

My bicycle arrived. Shortly afterwards I had punctures in both wheels caused by the inner tubes being nipped on assembly. This rather knocked the edge off my idea of a bespoke machine. I suppose it reminded me of the realities of retailing and of that old adage 'Anticipation is better than realisation'.

After work I would put the bike on the back of the car and drive into the countryside, seeking the quietest roads that I could find. Then I would practise. Slow-speed balance was a challenge. Sometimes I would struggle with gear selection, but I persevered.

One evening I was riding on a quiet rural road near to Harrogate when a large American car approached. I judged that passing would be difficult so I slowed and stopped. Despite frantic efforts, I was unable to get either of my feet free from the pedal cages. Slowly, I toppled onto a grass bank, where I lay helplessly at an acute angle.

The car stopped next to me and the window slid down. 'Excuse me sir,' said a very polite young American. 'Is there a military camp near here?'

I was lying on my left side in the riding position but I was able to lift my head and make eye contact. 'Yes, take the next left and it's about half a mile on the right.'

'Thank you, sir,' he said gravely. The window closed and he drove on.

I never was a natural rider. My 'Waterloo', as it could be called, came some weeks later. More confident now, I was making a fast but controlled descent of a long hill and a dangerous bend. It could have been the Pyrenees but this time it was the back road into Otley.

I was in high gear, head down and concentrating hard, when my new wife Sue passed me sitting upright on an old shopping bike which had three Derailleur gears and a basket on the front. The wind was in her hair and she was shouting gleefully.

Naturally, I talked with her about safety, but she seemed unimpressed and for some reason I felt a bit wimpish and a spoilsport.

A few weeks later I gave my bike to my son-in-law.

North Sea Crossing

At the end of the summer in 2016, I decided to bring *Juno* (our current motorboat) back from the Netherlands to England. She was due for a survey for insurance purposes at the end of 2017 and I knew that there would be some work to do prior to this. She would have to be out of the water and it would have been difficult, due to distances, for me to arrange this in the Netherlands.

Sue and I, with two friends who were both experienced seamen, travelled by ferry from Hull to Rotterdam. We then drove to Braassemermeer, just south of Amsterdam, where *Juno* has had her home mooring for some years. Later that day, Sue returned to England with the car whilst we three men stayed on *Juno* and prepared for the voyage.

On the first afternoon and the following morning we had a major engine service. Fuel was taken on board from a tanker moored at the end of the lake and after lunch we began our inland waterways journey to the port of Ijmuiden.

We travelled north through Amsterdam before turning west on the North Sea Canal that runs between Amsterdam and Ijmuiden, where we arrived at about 6pm. We moored in the huge Marina and bought our overnight ticket ready for departure the next day. By 7pm we had eaten. We were already tired but telephone calls from England alerted us to some bad weather, which was due to arrive over the following days.

The idea of being stranded in Ijmuiden was worrying. The cost was a factor, and all of us had expected to be home in a couple of days. We had a discussion and, though none of us really wanted to have a night crossing, we decided that it was the best option. We decided to set off immediately.

Depending upon the sea state, voyaging by night is not necessarily more hazardous than voyaging by day. Buoys and boats are well lit and, with modern instrumentation and up-to-date electronic charts, a huge amount of information – often more than one needs – is to hand.

Even so, things do go wrong. In our case it was an intermittent fault on our wheelhouse radio, which, though it never proved dangerous, caused some head scratching.

We left Ijmuiden in the dark, skirted the 'laying-up area' for large ships and headed west towards Lowestoft.

The journey is 100 nautical miles and at eight knots takes twelve and a half hours in good conditions.

When we were half an hour out of Ijmuiden John Hunter, who was on the wheel, spotted a large, official-looking vessel on our starboard side. It was grey and unmarked, on a similar course to us and some distance away. It came closer and was obviously tracking us. It looked threatening.

Rather nervously, I tried to raise it on the radio. 'Motor vessel *Juno* to unidentified vessel starboard side, over.'

No response.

'They're lowering a boat,' said John. 'It must be customs.' Soon a four-man dirigible came alongside. I opened the wheelhouse door.

'Throttle back to six knots,' came the shouted instruction. 'Permission to come aboard.'

I held out a hand to help but this was refused. (Later I realised that training would have included the possibility of suspect crew pushing a man into the water and speeding away.)

The man who climbed into the wheelhouse was enormous. With full deep-sea kit, and presumably body protection and weaponry, he filled the space. His assistant followed him whilst the sinister-looking black dirigible with two others on board maintained station alongside.

The man was very polite and to the point. I produced all my papers and answered questions whilst his companion searched the boat. At the end of the procedure, I asked if they were also looking for people. He told me that immigration would be responsible for that; normally, though not tonight, they would have had an immigration officer with them.

They left after about twenty minutes. The younger man made a rather unfortunate parting remark. He said, 'You are very brave to cross the sea tonight.'

The boarding had shaken us all enough without him saying that. We were not brave; only fools are brave at sea.

We had a difficult crossing. For much of the time we were on a quarter-beam sea, which was very uncomfortable. We were thrown about to the point where we felt sick; otherwise the voyage was uneventful. We arrived at Lowestoft mid to late morning. The last few miles, where we could see the land, seemed to take hours.

We radioed the harbourmaster to ask permission to enter harbour. We tried several times to raise him and eventually, having waited for rather a long time, we sneaked in and found a berth. Sometime later I found that the radio was faulty and I was able to apologise in person to the harbourmaster, though I don't think we had been noticed.

At Lowestoft we were weathered in for several days. A triathlon competition prevented us breaking our voyage at Wells-next-the-Sea as we had hoped so, when we left Lowestoft, we had a seventeen-hour journey to Grimsby. The following day we journeyed up the estuary to Goole and then finally home.

Limericks

I mentioned limericks earlier; here are two more. They are both quite gentle, maybe a little smutty, but hopefully amusing in an unsophisticated sort of way!

> A baker from Market Harborough,
> Took a girl that he fancied to Scarborough.
> He said, 'My dough's rising,
> It's scarcely surprising,
> It's under a cloth in the larder.'

Followed by:

> A butcher from Blackpool with bling,
> Inadvertently chopped off his 'thing'.
> It fell in the tray
> Where the sausages lay,
> So he tied it back on with brown string.

Finally, an incomplete one:

> A supple young gymnast from Luton,
> Was bearing her beau on her futon.

The second line could equally be: 'Was baring her 'bo' on her futon.'

Normally I try to rhyme the last line with the first two but in this case, I can't think of anything that rhymes other than crouton, or any two words ending in 'on' such as 'suit on'. Somebody suggested Putin, but I think that's a long stretch. None of which seem to be much help. So – a challenge!

Peter Peter

O ne of my earliest advertising commissions was to photograph an expensive 'gentleman's raincoat' worn by a model on location. The model was to be a distinguished looking man of middle years and on his arm would be an elegant lady. The location was a beauty spot near Halifax and the photograph was to be taken against the setting sun using the natural evening light.

The creative director who telephoned and briefed me was called Peter.

As was often the case, the budget was tight. I had worked previously with a model, also called Peter. He was perfect for this raincoat job: he was tall and good-looking, with chiselled features. The only problem was that he had another engagement in Hull that afternoon. Despite this, he was confident that he could get to my location in good time.

I was less confident. I knew that he wanted the job but I also knew that things can go wrong on photographic shoots and that a relatively short booking in the afternoon can often run on unexpectedly into the evening. I stressed the importance of my job and the fact that the setting sun meant that I didn't have any flexibility as to time. Peter was persuasive; despite my anxiety, and because he was the best man for the job, I booked him.

I arrived at the location with an assistant and a stylist in good time. Fortunately the weather was kind even though it was early in the spring. The female model arrived and looked wonderful. We rehearsed positions whilst we waited for Peter. We made test Polaroids. Everything was ready.

Peter did not arrive and the light was beginning to fade. I knew that we had very little time before it would be too dark. This was the first time that I had worked for this agency; I wanted to create a good impression and I was becoming more and more nervous by the minute. We were all getting cold, walking up and down the field and looking to the road for cars. I was panicking.

It is fair to say that I was truly agitated when a car pulled up. A man, whom I didn't recognise, ran across the field towards me. 'Peter couldn't make it. He's very sorry but he's sent me instead.'

I was so shocked that I abandoned normal courtesy and lambasted this poor man. I told him that he was woefully inadequate because he simply was not tall enough, that he wasn't handsome enough for the job, and that Peter had no right to assume that he could nominate a replacement. I went on and on in this vein for some minutes.

God knows what the poor man thought. He looked truly crestfallen. Although he was very shaken, he made a brave effort to justify his presence and said words to the effect that he had actually designed the advertisement and, though Peter the creative director had not been able to come – and though it was very short notice – he thought that he was probably good enough to 'art direct' in Peter's place.

There are moments when one feels that all is lost. This was one of them. Seconds later, Peter the model arrived and we were able to take the photograph in the dying moments of the light. As I recall, the photograph was adequate though not sensational. Location photography in England is invariably hit and miss because of the weather.

Over the years most of my work was studio-based where the stress factors, though still high, were more manageable.

Fishing with John

On an unseasonably cold and very wet night, a colleague called John and I were sitting on the bank of the River Lune fishing for salmon. Our original intention had been to fish for sea trout. On certain rivers, the Lune included, it is said that if you can see your hand in front of your face it is still too light for fishing. Sea trout are very shy and even a moonlit night can dramatically reduce the chances of success.

We had left Leeds in the early evening and driven several hours to this stretch of the river way above Kirby Lonsdale. We had not realised that the Lune would be in flood, nor had we realised that it would be raining. Fly-fishing was out of the question, so we decided to dig for a few worms and fish for salmon in the slack water. So there we were, fifty yards apart in the dark, determined not to waste our evening but feeling rather sorry for ourselves.

We didn't catch anything but I think that eels were nibbling at my worms, because I frequently recovered my tackle to find that I had a bare hook. Despite my considerable embarrassment I kept having to ask John if he would put another worm on my hook. Though it's not something I would choose to boast about, I cannot bear to touch worms.

Though it's not something that he would want everyone to know, John is scared of bats. He was uneasy. The air was thick with bats and, though I kept assuring him that they were swallows, I'm not sure that he was convinced.

Eventually, in the early hours of the morning, we decided to go home. We were wet, cold and tired.

The car was parked at the top of the field at least a quarter of a mile away. We trudged along the riverbank, John in the lead, me following. The ground was very uneven and our progress was slow. John thought that we had walked too far and missed the turn up the field towards the car. I knew that we would eventually reach a ditch, which was our cue to turn away from the river. John was not convinced and started to talk about us being completely lost in the middle of nowhere, not to be found for days.

It was very dark, the weather was foul, we were a long way from home and it was easy for the imagination to play tricks. We had a torch with a red filter, which was supposed to help night vision. John was using this, illuminating a small circular patch of ground immediately to his front. The disadvantage of a red filter is that it is a complementary colour to the green of the grass and makes it look grey, which is very spooky indeed.

We staggered on. Suddenly, without warning, John stopped, threw his arms in the air and gave the most terrible cry. He had walked into a sleeping cow, which lumbered to her feet in front of him. I crashed into his back, my heart lurching in my chest with the shock. Fishing tackle flew everywhere. The cow cantered away.

The journey home was uneventful, though both of us were probably wondering why we, of all the people that we knew, should have paid so much money to be quite so miserable when we could have been at home in a warm bed.

Selling the Saab

In the late 1980s it became necessary to sell my company car, a Saab Cabriolet. We advertised the car privately and some people from Manchester telephoned to say that they were interested. They arranged to come to my house that evening at about eight o'clock. It would be dark but it was not possible to come earlier as they were working.

The would-be purchasers arrived in a scruffy old car. That surprised me. What surprised me even more was that the passenger ran into my roadside back garden and hid in the bushes. Though it was dark, my initial impression was that the passenger was a large lady and that she was wearing a fur coat. I decided not to say anything.

The driver greeted me pleasantly and asked to see the car.

I opened the garage door. We walked around the car, which was parked against the side wall of the garage. 'Shall I move it so that you can see the other side?' I asked.

He said that wouldn't be necessary. I asked him if he would like to see inside the boot but that was also unnecessary. I asked if I should lift the bonnet; he said words to the effect that he was sure that there would be an engine in there, and he didn't need to see it. All this sounds as if he was quite terse but this was not the case. He was very pleasant and prepared to take everything at face value. Finally, he said, 'Good, we'll have it!'

We shook hands and he went to his car. He rummaged under the driver's seat and returned with a cloth bag full of used notes. He said, 'You can count it if you want but you'll find it's correct.' By this time, I had learned that he was a wholesale market trader. Even so, a bag with so many thousands of pounds in it and the knowledge that someone was still hiding in the garden resulted in me feeling extremely agitated.

Because the Saab was fitted with a telephone that would have to be removed by a garage, he couldn't take the car straight away. I explained this and said that the car would be ready for collection on the following evening. He was unhappy about having to drive over from Manchester a second time, but I promised him a tankful of petrol as recompense. With my apologies and a further handshake, the deal was done.

Before he left, he handed me the bag of money. 'Here, you have this.' This startled me and I became quite anxious. He was not taking the car and I thought that he would keep the money until the following evening.

Noting my discomfort, he said, 'What can be wrong? Think about it – you've got the money and the car.'

His passenger who, though indistinct in the darkness, now looked more like a man than a woman, sidled out from the bushes, got in the car and they drove away. I went back into the house, clutching the bag of money and wondering if I was the subject of an elaborate scam.

I was living alone at the time. That night I put the money bag under the bed and had a troubled sleep.

The following day I banked the money, which correct to the penny. The car was collected in the evening, at which time I learned that the passenger – who was indeed a man, in fact the driver's brother – was to be the new owner. He was extremely shy.

It seemed that everything was satisfactory. Well, nearly satisfactory.

Many months later, I happened to be in the reception area of my studio when a huge man came in through the front door. I asked if I could help and he said he was looking for Mr McBurney. He was a bailiff and, to my astonishment, he served me with a summons relating to non-payment of parking fines for a Saab car in Manchester.

I don't remember the details. There were several offences and, despite it no longer being my car, the only options that I had were to attend court or pay a considerable fine.

In the studio we were in the middle of one of our busiest periods of work; for me to attend court even for half a day would have meant standing down assistants, stylists and models, and would have cost the company a considerable loss in turnover.

The only thing of which I was guilty was naïveté in believing the purchasers when they said they would deal with the paperwork relating to the car. Despite the unfairness of the situation, we paid the fine. Fortunately we were able to make sure that ownership of the car was transferred satisfactorily.

In this case not so much buyer beware, but seller beware!

Diary

1st June–30th June 2018

June 2018

Friday 1st

Part of Hawksworth Wood used to be a quarry. On either side of the path there are huge pieces of cut stone. Many of the stones are beautiful or, if not beautiful, at least impressive because of their size and attractive because of the multicoloured lichen and stains on their surfaces. Unfortunately, one or two of them have been defaced by graffiti.

The graffiti made me think about cave paintings. I don't suppose that I am different from many other people in romantically imagining that cave paintings might be the result of some sensitive adult, full of wonderment about the natural world, making marks with primitive materials and possibly aware that, because of their sheltered position, the drawings might last for a very long time. Almost someone with a sense of history.

What if we are 'gilding the lily'? What if the artist was one more needy teenager and this was Stone Age graffiti?

I imagine a conversation that might have taken place in the cave. I don't know if the participants had language but, with or without it, a loose interpretation might be:

Mother: 'I wish you'd wash that off! It's dangerous enough outside without having a bison on our bedroom wall. Your dad will be home soon and he'll have something to say about it.'

Saturday 2nd
Overheard: 'Well, if he's folically challenged, what does it say about me? I must be really thick!'

Friday 8th
With some 'encouragement' from Sue, I have just had my eyes tested. There is a very small deterioration in the left eye, my 'bad' eye, but the right eye is just as it was a year ago with no change to my prescription. I'm trying to come to terms with the level of my relief but for the moment I just feel numb. As Yeats said in another context: 'For peace comes dropping slow.' I think that may be applicable to relief following long anxiety.

Earlier today, Ruby was perched on the edge of the pond in the courtyard with her bottom in the air and her nose on the water. The pond is built up with stone and finished off with Yorkshire-stone slabs that overhang the water. Hiding under the overhang was a bedraggled, newly-fledged blue tit. It was tweeting at the top of its voice, almost certainly calling for its parents. Ruby was beside herself with excitement. Her whole body was trembling as she tried to get at the bird.

I held her tightly and tried to reason with her. I told her that baby birds were not fair game. I know that it's nonsensical trying to reason with a dog, but some little part of me hoped that she might have felt able to spare this beautiful little baby bird. Not a bit of it. If anything, she became even more excited. I think that she thought I was there to join her in the hunt.

I locked Ruby in the house. I caught the bird and placed it in the bushes near to the nest. Its tail was wet but nothing more, so hopefully it will survive.

Anthony Bourdin died last night. I was in New York on business many years ago and, having read his books since then, I realise that I ate onion soup (the best onion soup I've ever had) in the bistro where he worked. Though I never met him, he enriched my life. He was a cook, a writer and a TV presenter. He was a big man in every sense, with a tremendous personality. When you read his books, you felt that you knew him; additionally you felt that he knew you and that he was talking to you directly.

Occasionally TV makes one realise how small the world is; without him, today it feels smaller. And sadder.

Sunday 17th

A few weeks ago, Ruby caught a baby squirrel. I didn't see it happen, I just heard the sound of her shaking something violently. When I came round the corner, she was trotting away and the squirrel was lying on the ground.

I haven't written about this until now; indeed, I have tried not to think about it. However, it has troubled me greatly. The squirrel was not dead but it probably had a broken neck and I had to kill it.

It was a beautiful little thing.

I won't go into further detail, other than to say I have struggled to understand how some people would think nothing of this. I meet sociable, friendly dog walkers who tell me proudly that their dogs kill rabbits and squirrels regularly. All of this makes me feel a bit of a wimp. I have a dog, she chases squirrels and when she catches one I wring my hands in horror. Double standard?

Monday 18th

Scam. A horrible word, a horrible experience.

On 27 April 2017 my computer crashed. A message flashed up: do not touch anything and ring this number (which purported to be Microsoft). The person who answered my call gave me a phone number, which he described as being their only accredited repair centre.

I made the call and was told that if I didn't act immediately, I was in danger of losing everything. I was particularly concerned about losing my photographs, some of which I was considering marketing as fine-art prints. This alone made me feel extremely vulnerable.

The salesman encouraged, cajoled and bullied me into buying a repair package which included a year's service. It was really expensive but I felt that I didn't have other options.

At the end of the transaction, the salesman said not once but several times that his company would never telephone me under any circumstances. He explained that this was for my security as it would prevent me from being duped by anyone else who might falsely claim to represent them. He went on to say that if I wanted to renew my contract at the end of the year, it would be up to me to contact them. This was all very reassuring.

Whether or not the circumstances that led to this contract were legitimate, the service that followed was helpful and professional. However, I didn't have any need to contact them during the final several months and I decided that I wouldn't renew.

A week ago, I received a call from the company. I didn't think it was an impostor because the caller was able to quote details. The caller insisted that I owed money to his company, that I had a contract over three years. When I protested, he said that he was happy to cancel my contract at the cost of some hundreds of pounds.

Over the course of a long conversation I was threatened with courts, with bailiffs, debt collectors and fines. I requested information in writing but this was not available.

After several calls I installed a call-blocking telephone system. The caller has continued to try to contact me using different names, but fortunately I have been able to recognise the voice and block him.

The Internet is full of scam stories about this company. Interestingly, some of the posts suggest that the children of older people are having difficulty in persuading their parents that they have been the subject of a scam. I empathise with this absolutely; it's quite difficult to admit that you have been fooled. The fact that part of the service that you have received has been professionally competent 'clouds' the possibility that you didn't need it in the first place, that you paid too much for it, and that you might continue to pay because you feel threatened.

This is an uncomfortable story about a horrible situation. It's uncomfortable not just for me but for anyone caught up in something similar. Until it happens, it is difficult to imagine how shaken one feels.

Buy the best computer protection that you can afford.

Saturday 30th

Sue and I have just returned from a week in Chichester and Brighton. Sue's father, who lives in Devon, was having a reunion meal in Chichester with former colleagues and suggested that we went down there to spend some time with him.

It's probable that none of us will ever forget the temperature during this last week. As a result, the amount of flesh on display in Chichester was breath-taking. An evening spent in South Street will live in the memory. I remember saying to Sue that mostly the people we saw were young or old, and the young were wearing very little and the old were wearing very much. Sue corrected me. She said that some of the old were also wearing very little, which she thought was even more terrifying!

Sue is a kind person and regrets saying that; I try to be kind, but I know what she meant.

Despite the fun of South Street, I felt uncomfortable with the ostentatious displays of wealth in the region. Village after village without a leaf out of place. This isn't just a whimsical observation; the differences between affluent areas of the South and most areas of the North are startling. I joked about the answers we might receive were we able to ask a representative number of people if they had an opinion about the north-south divide and the so-called Northern Powerhouse.

From Chichester we went to Brighton. Brighton is a 'proper' seaside town. Though it was midweek, everywhere was busy and parking was nearly impossible. Sue's brother, Mike, lives there in a shared house with an internal courtyard garden, a secret cool oasis. His home is in a multicultural area with a diverse selection of shops and restaurants. We were grateful for the experience of being there; it felt a little bit like home.

Whilst we were away, I relied on the *Guardian* website for news and I cannot be alone in finding this week so depressing. The continuing Windrush affair and the actions of the Home Office make me feel so ashamed. When Theresa May stood outside Number 10 in her opening address to the nation and spoke about serving all of the people, I really wanted to believe her. I suppose that the bitterness that I feel now is more acute because of my gullibility then.

This weekend ministers are meeting at Chequers in the hope of being able to put forward some unified proposals for our future relationship with Europe. In the meantime it seems that more and more people are obtaining citizenship of one of the seventeen states of the European Union. According to figures obtained by the BBC, in 2015 approximately 2,000 people obtained citizenship, increasing in 2016 to approximately 5,000, and in 2017 increasing to nearly 13,000. I wish that I was one of them. Sadly, I don't think that I qualify. It's not that I want to leave home, I would just like to continue travelling freely in Europe.

Memories

Recent

The Birthday Party

There are disadvantages to having been married three times, particularly if one is absent-minded. When Sue was sixty, we decided that we would book a large house somewhere and invite children and grandchildren for a long weekend.

We decided that Whitby was our place of choice and it was left to me to do the research and make a booking. Using the Internet, I found a large house near the museum in Whitby, which looked perfect.

I telephoned and had a very pleasant conversation with the proprietor. I explained our needs, our numbers and the nature of the occasion. She was helpful and I booked the property for the fifteenth of August. Everything went so smoothly, I was very pleased with myself.

When Sue came back, I told her of my achievement. She looked incredulous. 'What date did you say?'

Unfortunately, I had booked the house on Faye's birthday.

Under the circumstances, Sue was very gracious. She explained to me that she was younger than my previous wife Faye (all of seven days), and suggested that I changed the booking. At this point I experienced a little panic. I had made the booking a couple of hours earlier and, as it was for August, I feared that I might not be able to change it without a penalty. My worst fear was that it would be booked for the days I wanted.

I telephoned immediately. Fortunately all went well, though in fairness to the proprietor I felt the need to explain my reasons. She was very professional and quite charming. 'Of course I understand,' she said. 'It's the sort of thing that could happen to anyone.'

I could hear the edge of hysteria in her voice. 'Thank you so much,' I said, and put down the telephone.

Though she was in Whitby and I was in Leeds, I swear that I could hear her voice as she ran through her house looking for someone to tell and shouting, 'You will never guess what this man has just done!'

Exhibition

Last year a long-time friend, David McCallam, asked me if I would like to exhibit two of my 'beautiful prints' in an exhibition that he was organising in Hebden Bridge.

Initially I thought not. I didn't have any prints which were framed and available and, though I was flattered, I have only exhibited once before and that was nearly forty years ago when I was chair of the North Light Photographic Trust in Leeds. Since then, all of my photographic advertising work has been client-led and I have never tried to sell my own prints.

David persisted, explaining that the exhibition was several months ahead, that I had lots of time, and it would help him considerably. Naturally I was flattered.

David was clever. He waited until I had agreed in principle before telling me that there was a theme. I choked a bit at this. He explained that the theme was 'Industry'.

'I can't do it,' I said, because nearly all of my work is still life.

David continued to apply gentle pressure. 'It doesn't have to be taken too literally, it could be almost anything.'

I experienced that 'here we go again feeling'. I knew that I would leave everything to the last moment and then be in a panic.

David's final stroke was to tell me that there was an entry fee of £5. He also told me that all the organisation would be through Facebook. Fortunately, Sue is on Facebook and was able to keep me up to date.

As I feared, the weeks passed and the deadline was close. I decided to go down to the Leeds Industrial Museum, where I remembered having seen surplus pieces of machinery rusting away in the grounds at the back of the buildings.

I found some large riveted tanks and then some smaller machined castings with flaking red paint. I set up my tripod and camera and started to take pictures. It was raining gently. I must have looked quite professional simply because of the equipment I was using, so I was slightly bemused when a man pushing a bicycle stopped and asked, 'What you do?'

He seemed pleasant and sociable, so I explained something of my method. He listened for a moment and then interrupted me, 'You need sun.'

'No,' I said. 'This soft light is perfect for colour, and this soft rain is good because it gives flare to some of the flat surfaces and that adds interest to the picture.'

He thought for a moment and shook his head. 'No. You need sun and bucket water,' he said, and walked on.

Despite my reservations, I was pleased with my pictures and with the exhibition, which was held in The Birchcliffe Centre, a beautifully restored Methodist Church high on the hillside overlooking Hebden Bridge.

Turkey Soup

Maisie and I were early for her appointment with the consultant. We sat in the car and talked. Maisie had been having 'episodes', which Sue and I thought were probably diverticular. However, Maisie had different ideas about the cause and very little that we said seemed to have made any impression on her.

Some weeks earlier, Maisie had spent Christmas with Auntie Olive. Auntie Olive was a notoriously frugal woman; though not without considerable means, she wasted nothing. It seems that Auntie Olive had made soup from a turkey carcass which was several days old. Not only that, but there was sufficient soup to last for days.

Maisie told us that she had eaten the soup despite any anxieties that she had because, 'It was all there was. I had to eat it.' She was now convinced that Auntie Olive's turkey soup had poisoned her.

Within the family we had become heartily sick of this ongoing story about Auntie Olive's turkey soup but now, with time to spare before her appointment, I felt that I had to talk about it. I began hesitantly.

Almost immediately, I became aware that I was talking to her as if she was a child.

'Mum.'

'Yes, dear.'

'When you see the consultant, it would be best if you were able to let him express an opinion about your condition. What I mean is that he is the expert, and we've come to see what he thinks.'

Maisie was not charitable. 'Of course. I know that, Robert. Why did you think we were here? You don't have to tell me how to behave.'

The consultant presented immaculately. A perfect length of white cuff emerged from a beautifully cut dark suit. He sat at a traditional desk with matching furnishings. A Mont Blanc fountain pen lay on the leather-bound blotter.

There is no doubt that he was as perfect a specimen of the successful professional man as might be imagined. It occurred to me, rather unkindly, that if one spends part of one's days investigating the inner secrets of people's bottoms one might feel the need to dress like a princely merchant banker rather than sloshing around in a lab coat and rubber gloves.

After initial questioning, the consultant and a nurse took Maisie into a side room where she was examined. On her return, we sat in front of the consultant's desk and waited for him to speak. He concentrated on his notes for a time and then, lifting his Mont Blanc pen for effect, he paused and looked up.

Unable to contain herself a moment longer, Maisie leaned forward and said, 'Would *you* make soup from a five-day old turkey carcass?'

I watched him as she spoke, and there was no doubt that he was thrown off balance. I remember thinking, 'What an unfair question! This is a man who has never made soup.'

I believe that he was lost for words because Maisie was able to tell him the full story, which included additional detail about Auntie Olive's refusal to turn on the central heating and various other bits of information that she believed to be central to her case.

He sat with his head inclined to one side, smiling in sympathy and listening intently. At the end, after telling Maisie that he suspected a diverticular problem that would need to be confirmed by further testing, he was gracious enough to acknowledge the dangers that Maisie had experienced during her exposure to turkey soup.

As we returned to the car Maisie looked at me, not without an element of self-satisfaction. 'He knew,' she said. 'He knew.'

Maisie's Rose

Maisie

It is difficult to write about my mother as a younger woman. My earlier memories are clouded by more recent memories of the person she became in older age.

In her late eighties, she moved from lively independence to a care home and finally to a nursing home, where she lived for many years. I visited her once a week, but my sister Louise visited her and cared for her on an almost daily basis.

In her later years Maisie was very confused and unhappy. Railway stations played a large part in her fears. She would tell us that everyone had been locked in a station waiting room overnight, waiting for a train that never came. She would implore us to help her. No amount of reassurance gave her comfort.

At other times she believed that she was being moved from place to place without explanation. Sometimes she was terrified. She would shout for help, her tired old hands clawing at the air. Nothing consoled her.

Occasionally there were instances of dark humour.

Once, when I was talking to her, she said, 'Robert's coming today.'

'Yes,' I said. 'I'm Robert.'

She ignored this and we continued talking.

'Robert's coming today.'

Gently, I told her that I was Robert and yes, I had come to visit her. She ignored this also. We talked some more.

'Robert's coming today.'

I explained myself again. More directly – and quite irritably – as if she was speaking to a recalcitrant child, she said, 'Yes, I've heard you. So you're both here,' and we carried on talking.

Though she – and we – suffered during her final years, after her death I experienced terrible shame and anger.

Once, many years ago, she said to me, 'Robert, if ever I grow old and doolally will you hit me on the head with a hammer or something?' Of course I said yes, but she wasn't satisfied with a glib answer and she pressed me on the subject and made me promise to carry out her wish. I don't think for a moment that she did want me to hit her on the head, but I think she hoped that the 'or something' part of her wish might allow some action that would give her a peaceful and dignified end of life.

Of course she should never have asked, and I should never have agreed, but these things are said.

I suppose that I, as the eldest child, felt a burden of responsibility for her. Despite the fact that the law is clear and no options were available to us, I cannot escape from the fact that had she been any living creature other than human I would have been censored for keeping her alive in such a distressed state of mind and body.

Her death was unnecessarily long. The human body takes some weeks to close down.

I think that it is a shocking reflection on our society that, quite unnecessarily, we continue to allow some people to die in misery and fear. Believe it or not, it happens in the name of God. In my opinion it is appalling. Simple common sense and simple common decency should allow us to have control over our own lives. Death can be kind and *should* be kind. No one is suggesting that there is a simple solution that is appropriate in all cases, but there must be 'better ways' and we must find them.

Diamond and Maya

One of the photographs of the dogs that I took at Marcus's is quite striking. Two heads together, but anxiety in their eyes, particularly Maya. I have learned that animals are uncomfortable when stared at directly.

On holiday in Spain many years ago, I was sitting in the fork of a lemon tree drawing three horses. Slowly they moved away from me until they were at the far end of the field. Unable to see them sufficiently to carry on drawing I turned and, facing in the opposite direction, began to draw the landscape. After five minutes or so I felt a bump in my back and turned to see three horses who couldn't have been closer to me, and who were obviously very interested in what I was doing.

Bach

When the children were studying, I gave each of them a boxed LP of Arthur Grumiaux playing Bach's sonatas and partitas for solo violin, with instructions to listen to the great Chaconne in 'Partita Number Two' whenever the going got really tough.

Of course, being young and wise they thought I was 'just a bit' mad. I seem to remember that they were kind to me because they knew I meant well, but they were obviously unconvinced. I'm quite pleased, twenty-five years later, to see the very LP standing in the corner of Marcus's living room. Admittedly it's a bit dusty but, as they say, it's the thought that counts.

The Wart

Recently I had a wart removed from my chin. When it first appeared, I thought that it was a spot and that it would disappear with time. I did the usual things that one does with a spot: dabs of antiseptic cream, a bit of judicious squeezing. Unfortunately this seemed to encourage growth in the way that watering and tending might do with a plant. As it grew, I realised that this spot was actually a wart. Not just any old wart, but a wart with ambition.

I began to apply a proprietary ointment designed to burn the wart and eventually stop it in its tracks. Though it caused some damage, the wart fought back. In desperation I used a pair of nail clippers and cut it off. This is not a recommended treatment. It bled copiously; it hurt a lot.

Though the wart had suffered a setback, it made a recovery. I mentioned it to the doctor when visiting on another matter. He referred me to the practice nurse.

Over an extended period, I made several visits to the practice nurse. Each time I saw her, she froze the wart by pressing the spout of a canister against it. Towards the end, she was almost kneeling on my chest to try and get her weight behind the canister to achieve maximum penetration. We got to know each other quite well, and my visits were not without humour, but eventually we had to admit defeat and she referred me back to the doctor.

The doctor telephoned me and told me that he would make an appointment with a local surgery where minor surgical procedures were conducted.

On the morning of my appointment, I went to the barber's to have my beard trimmed. It occurred to me that the surgeon might require me to shave the relevant area of my chin and so I asked for a 'number one' which is the shortest cut.

I had an interesting conversation with the hairdresser. She told me that some years ago she had had several warts on her neck that had been frozen and excised by laser. This was quite reassuring. She also told me that in years gone by she would probably have been my surgeon, because barbers were the only people on the high street with sharp blades. She went on to explain that the red-and-white pole is symbolic of blood and dressings. I was pleased that things have moved on.

I went to my appointment hoping, and half expecting, that I would have the freezing and laser treatment.

The surgeon was charming. He came out into the reception to greet me and we chatted pleasantly as we walked to the surgical area. Understandably I was nervous though, being a man, I tried to disguise it by being rather jolly and over-garrulous. As instructed, I lay on the couch. In a futile effort to retain some vestige of control over matters, I mentioned my earlier conversation about freezing and lasers.

'That must have been a very posh place,' he said. 'We only have a soldering iron.'

The procedure involved an injection in the wart, which stung for a moment, followed by 'burning out' with the 'soldering iron'. The smell so close to one's nose was horrible, but the whole procedure was efficient and pain-free.

It may be my imagination but warts, like verrucas, seem to be very mysterious things. Sometimes they fall out, sometimes they disappear; they are unpredictable. For some reason, which I will never know, my chin was chosen and I was the unwilling host to one of them. My chin has healed, leaving just a little bump under the skin, but they may be out there watching me and planning their next move.

Diary

3rd July–12th July 2018

July 2018

Tuesday 3rd

What a joy that the twelve boy footballers and their coach have been found alive and seemingly well, after being trapped underground in a Thai cave for nine days because of rising flood water.

I've just watched the first video footage taken, I think, by the two British divers who found them. It is very moving. Young boys – the youngest, we are told, only eleven years of age – are perched on a rough rock, in the dark, with deep water only a few feet below them. They are huddled together, dazzled by the light of the torch. They must be exhausted, hungry and frightened. Even so, there is no sign of panic. Collectively, because it's impossible to know who is speaking, they are courteous and grateful, even to the extent of saying 'Thank you very much' and 'See you tomorrow' as the two divers prepare to turn off the light and leave them.

Nearly eighteen million people have watched this footage. Now, we must wait. Experts are saying that the boys might have to stay underground for months until the rainy season has passed and water levels have dropped.

Despite the real fears for the lives of these boys, I can't get it out of my head that they are a football team. Our grandson Charlie, who is ten, is living and dreaming, eating and sleeping this football World Cup; I bet, given happier circumstances, that these boys would be exactly the same.

I had forgotten how passionate children can be.

I hope, as we all must, that a successful rescue happens soon; I also hope that the world football authorities do something wonderful by way of compensation for this bunch of lovely skinny kids and their unlikely named 'Wild Boar' football team.

Wednesday 4th

I watched the England–Colombia football match last night whilst Sue, unable to bear the tension, watched something else in the bedroom. And what tension it was.

Years ago Bill Shankly, the famous Liverpool manager, said words to the effect that, 'Some people think that football is a matter of life and death; well, they're wrong, it's much more important than that!'

Last night, it was almost true.

The match was shown on ITV and went to penalties. The tension racked up throughout the penalty shootout, leading to the very last kick which won the game for England.

Later, Sue and I watched *Match of the Day* on the BBC. The pundits were ecstatic. They had been filmed during the penalty shootout and I can't remember ever having seen such joy and relief from grown men either on TV or in life. Their joy was unfettered. For a few glorious moments everything else was forgotten; they hugged and danced and shouted and laughed. To watch them was to share their joy.

Friday 6th

Whilst we were in Brighton, there was a terrible car crash in Horsforth and a number of young people were killed and injured. Walking and talking with Diane this morning, I realise what a profound shock this has been not only for the families involved but also for the entire community. Diane has three sons and, as a family, they knew at least two of the boys who died. I do not know anyone who was involved and it is not proper for me to talk about it, other than to say that the loss of child is the saddest thing that one can imagine.

Yesterday I spent most of the day in the A&E department of Saint James's Hospital (known to most people in Leeds as Jimmy's). In the morning, I had a fall. It was probably to do with a drop in blood pressure. The reason for the fall wasn't immediately obvious and I mention my visit only because I want to acknowledge how thorough the staff at the hospital were. It would have been easy to send me home after a couple of hours, but they were insistent on crossing all the Ts and dotting all the Is. It's impossible to overvalue or over praise their degree of professionalism, but happily for us it's what they do time and time again.

It feels unseemly to mention my own small experience so soon after writing about a fatal accident but yesterday was the seventieth birthday of the NHS. Though there wasn't any evidence of partying in A&E, I was grateful to spend the day with them.

Another tragic incident. A volunteer diver involved in the cave rescue in Thailand has died. When the children were found, despite all the obvious difficulties in bringing them to the surface, one felt a degree of euphoria. It was as if everything had to turn out right in the end. I think that now the euphoria has gone and the death of a professional diver has underlined the danger and complexity of the rescue mission. We hope and wait.

Saturday 7th

I've been thinking about the significance of physical contact – human touch – in our lives and how much we take it for granted until it is lost to us with age.

In the womb, one might say that touch is constant. Certainly after birth, when we are babies and then children, hugs and cuddles are the norm. As young adults and young lovers, we experience a great deal of touch. As parents of young children, much the same.

As older adults I think we begin to experience less touch and, when we are very old, most touch comes from professional care rather than affection or intimacy.

In many cases I think that older people experience the lack of physical contact as a great loss. I remember saying goodbye to my brother after one of my regular – if infrequent – visits. It wasn't a moment of great significance, though his situation was always fairly desperate. He put his arms round me and hugged me as if his life depended upon it. I thought that his hug communicated things in a way that words could not.

I know that some people are less tactile than others and that I am talking in generalities; even so, it seems to me that, either through nature or nurture, physical human contact and touch is something that we need instinctively.

Many years ago, I heard someone use the expression 'dirty old man' about an older man who, in a domestic situation, kept touching a much younger woman on the arm and back. The touching was inappropriate only in as much as it was unwelcome. The young woman was uncomfortable with the situation and wanted to get away from him. I still respect her feelings but now that I am that 'older man' I can feel sorry for him. Let us say that I can empathise with the probable innocence of his need. It may be the way of the world, certainly the way of the animal kingdom, for old lions to be ostracised but a wish to make contact with youth and beauty is understandable, even if unwelcome. It is the stuff of life. To equate an instinctive desire for physical contact with the word 'dirty' seems unfair.

I'm not sure where this is leading me in this troubled time of male–female relationships. I just wonder how it would be if you, dear reader, as a beautiful young thing of a certain maturity seeing an old chap gazing at you wistfully, were to go up to him and say, 'Could I give you a hug?' I think that if you asked nicely, he might say yes. I also think that he would never forget the moment.

Possibly this concept could give birth to a 'Hug a Great-Grandad Day'.

That would get us all out on the streets.

Just an idea.

Monday 9th

What a day. We woke to the news that David Davies had resigned. Later, we learned that, thankfully, four more boys have been rescued from the cave in Thailand. Now Sue has just come in and told me that Boris Johnson has resigned.

These must be the most extraordinarily bitter times at Westminster. We know that the measured words of resignation letters and the spoken thanks for past support disguise intensities of feeling, anger and betrayal, the like of which we can only imagine. What comes next? It matters enormously to us all.

Eight pm. I've been watching the news channels and someone has just said that FIFA have invited the children from the Wild Boar football team to the finals of the World Cup if they are well enough to attend. It seems that the rescue attempt of the final four children and their coach will take place tonight and tomorrow. How wonderful it would be if they were all safe and well enough to attend the final. I think that people throughout the world would think it an appropriate and perfect end to an extraordinary drama.

Tuesday 10th

Wonderful, wonderful news. All the boys and their coach are safely out of the cave. A huge effort by an international team. As I write, the doctor and some of the divers who stayed with the boys are still to emerge; we hope that they do so safely.

More than a thousand people have been involved in this rescue. For them, this experience will be life changing.

For we who have watched and waited, it's such a shame that the relief felt by so many of us worldwide will not be able to find a voice. At this moment I am almost certainly just one of hundreds of millions of people who would love to reach out and share our relief and our joy with others outside our immediate families. The evidence is there; given the opportunity and the stimulus, individuals can pull together irrespective of race or religion or nationality. It is reassuring as well as being heart-warming.

Thursday 12th

I'm cheating a little bit, because I am starting to write this diary page and thinking about what I want to say a few days before the due date. I'm doing this because I would like to conclude this book with laughter and, realising that this is unlikely (particularly as Trump is arriving on my birthday), I would like to leave it – and you –with a smile at least.

In a few days it will be my seventy-ninth birthday, which means that I will begin my eightieth year.

When other people, usually older than me, tell me their age I sometimes respond by saying, 'Well, that's very careless of you. How did you let that happen?'

In my own case, I have also been careless because age does seem to have sneaked up on me. The real surprise is that this is one of my happiest times.

I'm lucky. I'm no longer working, with all the stress that work involves. I'm not as 'driven' as once I was and the result is that I have time for reflection; even occasionally time to do nothing. Selfish time, one could say, but time to try and behave better! Finally, I have many interests as well as having a dog which, as they say, gets me out.

As you will have realised from my writing, I have always been insecure. Presumably this is a legacy of my childhood. Now that I am older with, as one might say, nothing to lose, I feel able to talk about it without embarrassment or shame. Writing this book has been a help. It has made me think about my family, relationships, my own behaviour. There is no doubt that this has been therapeutic. Emotionally I feel more secure now than I felt previously. I mention this because it's comforting that things can get better so late in life and I cannot imagine that I'm alone in this respect.

As this is the last page, and assuming that you have read everything that has gone before, you probably know nearly as much about me as I know about myself. So if there are morals here, hopefully you will have found them.

On a lighter note I'll end with this story.

A month ago, I went to a friend's eightieth birthday. As he cut the cake, he quoted Oscar Wilde: 'With age comes wisdom, but sometimes age comes alone.'

I was left with the feeling that, in my case, things might come down to a choice: crumbs of wisdom or crumbs of cake.

If push comes to shove (a bit like Jo Brand), I'll probably take the cake.

Thanks

Thank you, Sue, for encouragement and support, often given at moments of my own self-doubt and undeniably fundamental to the progress of this book. Thank you, James Nash; friend, poet; for generous professional advice, unstintingly given. Thank you, sister Louise, for the hours that you spent sitting at this machine, sorting me out, technically and literally.

Thank you, son-in-law Sam, Stevie Frost, and Pat Gray for putting love and friendship at risk by asking to read my manuscript. Your approval gave me the courage to place it in the hands of professionals.

Thank you Jacob Boston for allowing me to use your pictures of Stewart Lowdon's paintings.

Finally, thank you everyone at 2QT publishing.

To Catherine, whose wisdom, patience and good humour allowed me to forego the vellum, the illuminations and the hand beaten gold trimmings.

To Karen, editor, with whom I shared some amusing emails, and who eventually forgave me for assuming that her reference to the pluperfect was a way of telling me that she thought my writing was extra special.

To Charlotte, designer, who laughed when first she read my design brief, *'When someone holds this book, I would like the fingers to caress it, the lips to smile and the heart to say, you belong to me, I will never let you go'*, and then proceeded to give me exactly that.

Thank you all, I'm truly grateful.